Getting the Buggers to Learn in FE

Getting the Buggers to Learn in FE

Dealing with the headaches and realities of college life

ANGELA STEWARD

continuum

Continuum International Publishing Group

The Tower Building   80 Maiden Lane,
11 York Road   Suite 704
London   New York
SE1 7NX   NY 10038

www.continuumbooks.com

© Angela Steward 2008

British Library Cataloguing-in-Publication Data
A catalogue record for this book is available from the British Library.

ISBN: 9–7808–2649–5679 (paperback)

Library of Congress Cataloging-in-Publication Data
Steward, Angela.
   Getting the buggers to learn in FE: dealing with the headaches and realities of college life/Angela Steward.
      p. cm. – (Essential FE toolkit series)
   ISBN-13: 978-0-8264-9567-9 (pbk.)
   ISBN-10: 0-8264-9567-2 (pbk.)
      1. Continuing education–Great Britain. 2. Adult learning–Great Britain. I. Title. II. Series.

   LC5256.G7S75 2008
   374.41–dc22

2007043787

Typeset by BookEns Ltd, Royston, Herts.
Printed and bound in Great Britain by MPG Books, Cornwall

Contents

Introduction

Chapter 1 Why is getting students to learn a problem?

Chapter 2 What are the problems in getting students motivated?

Chapter 3 *What are the problems in creating a learning environment?*

Chapter 4 *Why are theories about students' learning considered a problem?*

Chapter 5 *What are the problems with learning from a student's perspective?*

Chapter 6 *Why are teachers so important for students' learning?*

Chapter 7 Why are things always changing?

Conclusion

Dedication

To my family and friends from whom I learn so much about life and especially to my grandsons Jon and Josh – wishing them a happy life ahead.

Acknowledgements

Special thanks to students and colleagues in City College Norwich School of Education Studies who collaborated in my research, Jill Jameson for her editorial expertise and Alexandra Webster at Continuum for her encouragement.

Series Foreword

In the autumn of 1974, a young woman newly arrived from Africa landed in Devon to embark on a new life in England. Having travelled half way round the world, she still longed for sunny Zimbabwe. Not sure what career to follow, she took a part-time job teaching EFL to Finnish students. Enjoying this, she studied thereafter for a PGCE at the University of Nottingham in Ted Wragg's Education Department. After teaching in secondary schools, she returned to university in Cambridge, and, having graduated, took a job in ILEA in 1984 in adult education. She loved it: there was something about adult ed. that woke her up, made her feel fully alive, newly aware of all the lifelong learning journeys being followed by so many students and staff around her. The adult community centre she worked in was a joyful place for diverse multi-ethnic communities. Everyone was cared for, including 90-year-olds in wheelchairs, toddlers in the crèche, ESOL refugees, city accountants in business suits and university-level graphic design students. In her eyes, the centre was an educational ideal, a remarkable place in which, gradually, everyone was helped to learn to be who they wanted to be. This was the Chequer Centre, Finsbury, EC1, the 'red house', as her daughter saw it, toddling in from the crèche. And so began the story of a long interest in further education that was to last for many years. . . . Why, if they did such good work for so many, were FE centres so under-funded and unrecognised, so under-appreciated?

It is with delight that, 32 years after the above story began, I write the Foreword to *The Essential FE Toolkit*, Continuum's new book series of 24 books on further education (FE) for teachers and college leaders. The idea behind the *Toolkit* is to provide a comprehensive guide to FE in a series of compact, readable books. The suite of 24 individual books are gathered together to provide the practitioner with an overall FE toolkit in specialist, fact-filled volumes designed to be easily accessible, written by experts with significant knowledge and experience in their individual fields. All of the authors have in-depth understanding of further education. But – *'Why is further education important? Why does it merit a whole series to be written about it?'* you may ask.

At the Association of Colleges Annual Conference in 2005, in a humorous speech to college principals, John Brennan said that, whereas in 1995 further education was a 'political backwater', by 2005 FE had become 'mainstream'. John recalled that, since 1995, there had been '36 separate Government or Government-sponsored reports or white papers specifically devoted to the post-16 sector'. In our recent regional research report (2006) for the Learning and Skills Development Agency, my co-author Yvonne Hillier and I noted that it was no longer 'raining policy' in FE, as we had described earlier (Hillier and Jameson, 2003): there is now a torrent of new initiatives. We thought, in 2003, that an umbrella would suffice to protect you. We'd now recommend buying a boat to navigate these choppy waters, as it looks as if John Brennan's 'mainstream' FE, combined with a tidal wave of government policies will soon lead to a flood of new interest in the sector, rather than end anytime soon.

There are good reasons for all this government attention on further education. In 2004/05, student numbers in LSC council-funded further education increased to 4.2m, total college income was around £6.1 billion, and the average college had an annual turnover of £15m. Further education has rapidly increased in national significance regarding the need for ever greater achievements in UK education and skills training for millions of learners, providing qualifications and workforce training to feed a UK national economy hungrily in competition with other OECD nations. The 120 recommendations of the Foster Review (2005) therefore in the main encourage colleges to focus their work on vocational skills, social inclusion and achieving academic progress. This series is here to consider all three of these areas and more.

The series is written for teaching practitioners, leaders and managers in the 572 FE/LSC-funded institutions in the UK, including FE colleges, adult education and sixth form institutions, prison education departments, training and workforce development units, local education authorities and community agencies. The series is also written for PGCE/Cert Ed/City & Guilds Initial and continuing professional development (CPD) teacher trainees in universities in the UK, USA, Canada, Australia, New Zealand and beyond. It will also be of interest to staff in the 600 Jobcentre Plus providers in the UK and to many private training organisations. All may find this series of use and interest in learning about FE educational practice in the 24 different areas of these specialist books from experts in the field.

Our use of this somewhat fuzzy term 'practitioners' includes staff in the FE/LSC-funded sector who engage in professional practice in governance, leadership, management, teaching, training, financial and administration services, student support services, ICT and MIS technical support, librarianship, learning resources, marketing, research and development, nursery and crèche services, community and business support, transport and estates management. It is also intended to include staff in a host of other FE services including work-related training, catering, outreach and specialist health, diagnostic additional learning support, pastoral and religious support for students. Updating staff in professional practice is critically important at a time of such continuing radical policy-driven change, and we are pleased to contribute to this nationally and internationally.

We are also privileged to have an exceptional range of authors writing for the series. Many of our series authors are renowned for their work in further education, having worked in the sector for thirty years or more. Some have received OBE or CBE honours, professorships, fellowships and awards for contributions they have made to further education. All have demonstrated a commitment to FE that makes their books come alive with a kind of wise guidance for the reader. Sometimes this is tinged with world-weariness, sometimes with sympathy, humour or excitement. Sometimes the books are just plain clever or a fascinating read, to guide practitioners of the future who will read these works. Together, the books make up a considerable portfolio of assets for you to take with you through your journeys in further education. We hope the experience of reading the books will be interesting, instructive and pleasurable and that experience gained from them will last, renewed, for many seasons.

It has been wonderful to work with all of the authors and with Continuum's UK Education Publisher, Alexandra Webster, on this series. The exhilarating opportunity of developing such a comprehensive toolkit of books probably comes once in a lifetime, if at all. I am privileged to have had this rare opportunity, and I thank the publishers, authors and other contributors to the series for making these books come to life with their fantastic contributions to FE.

Dr Jill Jameson
Series Editor
March, 2006

Series Introduction

Getting the Buggers to Learn in FE –
Angela Steward

Angela Stewart, author of the highly successful *Survival Guide for Lecturers in FE* and *How to Teach in FE with a Hangover*, amongst other works, now turns her hand to tackle an age-old question – how do you facilitate student learning effectively? Why is learning sometimes such a problem for FE students? How can lecturers motivate students? What are the barriers to learning in the learning and skills sector? These and more are some of the issues Angela explores with us in this practical, evidence-informed guide to the facilitation of student learning, drawing from her 30 years' experience as a lecturer in FE.

Over the years I have read a wide range of literature about student learning. During various labyrinthine investigations, I strongly remember coming across a journal article that was a revelation to me at the time. In it, the author, a renowned US professor of educational psychology, summed up the entire history of learning theory in one simple sentence: *'After 100 years, we still don't really know how or why students learn.'* The blunt truth of this statement impressed me greatly, in contrast to those works trying to 'sell' their own ideas, more or less effectively, as unique 'solutions' to 'the student learning problem'. Reflecting on that article, I have ever since maintained an open, pragmatic approach to learning theory, recognizing our relative ignorance in this field, despite the many thousands of published theoretical works in it and despite the fact that, as Angela reminds us, learning is as natural as 'breathing or walking'.

xiii

I am therefore impressed by the stance that Angela takes to the tricky problem of motivating student learning in this book. She sagely observes us that, '...you can't make anyone learn, you can't cause learning to happen. But it's not all doom and gloom, you can create conditions which give learning a chance!' To create such conditions, Angela encourages us to be open to learning ourselves in order to be able to nurture learning in others. So, pragmatically, even if we accept that we don't *really* always know why or how students are learning, we need to be open to the fact that some principles *are* proven to work, some learning theories *are* useful, and some teaching and learning techniques can help in the struggle to help students achieve. Angela outlines a number of these useful techniques in this realistic, effective guide.

In Chapter 1, she introduces this book, questioning why getting students to learn is such a problem and recommending that we build on classroom discussions with students about the 'natural' learning they achieve all the time. In Chapter 2, she investigates problems with motivating students, recommending methods of achieving success in this, and noting the importance of feedback and praise. In Chapter 3, she discusses and analyses ways of creating positive learning environments, while Chapter 4 outlines a range of useful learning theories and research on learning. Chapter 5 looks at learning from students' perspectives, drawing on data from discussions with students. Chapter 6 reinforces the important role of teachers in FE, suggesting successful strategies for the creation of supportive learning environments. Chapter 7 queries why things are always changing, examining the role of FE teachers in relation to change and recommending that teachers themselves need to learn to keep up with and adapt to ongoing changes. In the Conclusion, Angela focuses on 'what matters', providing adaptable, helpful guidelines to 'get the buggers to learn' that teachers can interpret for their own situation.

This practical guide provides invaluable support and information for FE lecturers, trainers and others with student-focused responsibilities in the learning and skills sector who need to understand the complex issues involved in enabling improvements in student learning. Angela's specialist knowledge of FE and of the wider learning and skills sector make this an exceptionally useful work which will assist in helping many generations of students and teachers to learn in FE. I commend it highly to you.

Dr Jill Jameson
Director of Research and Enterprise
School of Education and Training
University of Greenwich
PhD, MA (King's College, London),
MA (Goldsmith's), MA (Cantab.), PGCE (Nottingham)

Glossary

EMA   Education Maintenance Allowance

ESOL   English for Speakers of Other Languages

FE   Further Education

GCSE   General Certificate of Secondary Education

ILP   Individual Learning Plan

LDD   Learning difficulty or disability

LSC   Learning and Skills Council

LSDA   Learning and Skills Development Agency

LSN   Learning and Skills Network

Ofsted   Office for Standards in Education

QIA   Quality Improvement Agency for Lifelong Learning

TLRP   Teaching and Learning Research Programme

VLE   Virtual Learning Environment

ZPD   Zone of Proximal Development

INTRODUCTION

Getting to know your students

> ... the FE learning experience is not simply a linear process, about passing exams, getting qualifications and a good job, despite their importance for many students ... Students also want to enjoy their learning and to be able to balance their studies with other personal priorities, be these economic survival, living independently, supporting a family, doing an existing job or, for many students, sustaining a vibrant lifestyle and becoming 'somebody'.
>
> (Gleeson, 2005: 241)

The purpose of this book is to help you understand that 'getting the buggers to learn in FE' is not simply about what happens to students in college, but about recognizing that students are only in college for part of the day and that it is 'no wonder families, friends, relationships, TV, film, computer games, music, fashion, sport, etc. are important to them' (Pollard, 2002: 84) as they are to students anywhere. Getting students to learn means getting to know your students, working with an understanding of the culture of students and realizing that you can use this to draw students into college work and make it an enjoyable experience. However, this sometimes means having to contend with students' other priorities and encouraging them to persevere with college work when their vibrant lifestyle beckons. Helping students to achieve what they want and reach their potential by making learning an enjoyable experience for them often means extra work for you as an FE teacher and – just like your students – you have to learn to change and adapt to survive in the classroom.

Every FE teacher you listen to at the moment seems to be talking about how things are changing in the Learning and Skills Sector of education in the UK. However, if you listen carefully, they don't all appear to be talking about the same things. Some are concerned about how to manage younger learners who are still at school and attend college for vocational subjects for just part of the week. Others are wondering how they'll achieve better results in GCSEs and A levels when they have less time in the classroom with learners. Many say how de-motivating it is for them when their learners only seem to be interested in collecting their Educational Maintenance Allowance rather than in the opportunity to learn or gain a qualification. The growth of Foundation Degrees in the sector has left many FE teachers anxious about how to prepare their learners for progression to an honours degree. Others are worried about the employability of their learners or whether there are enough opportunities out there anyway in their vocational line of work.

Whether it is concerns about teaching learners whose first language is not English, or those who are disenchanted, aggressive, indifferent, apathetic, need social care and special attention or are demanding and ambitious, all these concerns can stretch the patience of the most dedicated FE teacher and drain the enthusiasm of even the keenest new recruits to the Learning and Skills Sector.

Yet all these different concerns are a shared expression not only of the how things are changing in the sector but also of the problems and issues these changes create in such a diverse sector, and how they impact on the way learners learn and FE teachers teach. It is to be expected that if the characteristics and backgrounds of the learners you teach change and the conditions for learning in colleges change, then FE teachers need to change their practice. The trouble is that changing practice demands development time and this is just what FE teachers say they lack: time for creative and innovative curriculum development. Paperwork, meetings, verification processes and course management all encroach on non-teaching hours and often leave FE teachers feeling tired and exhausted – rather than feeling creative and innovative!

The consequences of not attending to changes and taking into consideration the need to change practices mean that FE teachers are storing up problems for themselves: learners become more disenchanted and teaching becomes more stressful. If this happens, both learners and teachers tend to take the line of least resistance and classrooms tend to become more conservative and formal with less personal interaction. I know that an FE teacher cannot cause learning or make anyone learn, but as Stenhouse

(1967) revealed many years ago, the teacher's task is not to cause learning but to control the direction of learning and the creative teacher is happy when learners are moving in a worthwhile direction. There is no definitive guidance from researchers and theorists on the most effective way or ways of encouraging worthwhile learning according to Tight (2000), but he indicates that researchers who have developed alternative approaches to learning theory, such as Marton, Hounsell and Entwistle (1984), have based their findings on listening to learners and what they say about what happens when they are studying.

With Tight's advice in mind, I have listened not only to what learners in FE say about how they learn, but also to what FE teachers say about how their learners learn and what they do to encourage learning – or as Stenhouse suggests, to control the direction of learning. In this book, I have also included with these findings examples of successful strategies identified by FE teachers and incorporated findings from other theorists that are relevant to learning in FE, and present them in this volume for FE teachers to pick up and consult when they are in need of ideas and reassurance as they face challenging groups.

Overview of chapters

As an FE teacher, I know that time is precious and I give below an outline of the chapters so that you can readily find what might be relevant to you. Each chapter poses a question that needs to be asked in relation to getting students to learn, and within the chapter there are activities to try out. At the end of each chapter there is a set of strategies to review which summarize the chapter contents.

CHAPTER 1 – Why is getting students to learn a problem? The importance of getting students talking about learning and getting organized is discussed.

CHAPTER 2 – What are the problems in getting students motivated? The subject of this chapter is how to achieve success and includes ways of getting students motivated and the importance of feedback and praise.

CHAPTER 3 – What are the problems in creating a learning environment? This chapter focuses on the importance of physical resources and provides an opportunity to evaluate your own teaching area. Key problems, for example, poor relationships with colleagues and organizational constraints, are addressed. The chapter includes an analysis of the learning environment – both educational and organizational.

CHAPTER 4 – Why are theories about students' learning considered a problem? The argument presented in this chapter is that the way FE teachers practice is underpinned by theories (even if they cannot be readily expressed), and that such ways can be developed through awareness of relevant learning theories and contemporary research. Understanding theories and how and why they work can help FE teachers to make decisions about how to modify and adapt such theories to get their students to learn.

CHAPTER 5 – What are the problems with their learning from a student's perspective? This chapter focuses on students and draws on data gathered from talking and listening to students, as getting students to learn requires access to the learners' perspective. There is an assumption that learning is the same for all and this chapter will explore how students, from a range of subject areas and levels, view learning and look at learning in current, everyday, real situations.

CHAPTER 6 – Why are FE teachers so important? It is a mistake to think that the use of innovative teaching methods – or new technology – will get students to learn; they often react differently from the way FE teachers predict. Getting students to learn is not just in the control of students but can be influenced by the approach FE teachers take to teaching, learning and structuring assessments. The FE teacher's role is to create a supportive learning environment. The FE teacher's subject expertise and professional delivery is at the core of getting students to learn as students cannot learn devoid of context.

Successful strategies that teachers use are provided to reinforce the idea that each subject area requires a different approach.

CHAPTER 7 – Why are things always changing? A brief look at the contemporary context and an evaluation of recent changes is provided. The argument presented here is that change is best dealt with by getting FE teachers to learn themselves!

CONCLUSION – Focusing on what matters. Although it cannot be thought of as a set of rules that if followed will inevitably get students to learn – the summary of ideas presented throughout the book are collated as a set of guidelines for you to adapt and actively interpret for your own context. FE teachers need a range of approaches for getting students to learn – it is not about choosing between one or another but being able to draw on a repertoire of skills and knowledge, and most importantly, focusing on what matters.

The rationale behind the book is that the absence of student learning is capable of being remedied. This book draws on a wide range of theories about students' learning but aims to be a practical guide to getting students to learn and provides positive remedies for the FE teacher which have been identified from talking to students and listening to successful FE teachers.

1

WHY IS GETTING STUDENTS TO LEARN A PROBLEM?

In this chapter you will find that getting students to learn is a problem because:

- Your learning agenda and the students' learning agenda are not necessarily the same;
- Students don't always realize they learn 'naturally' all the time;
- You can't make anyone learn.

You'll also find ideas about how to deal with these problems and how to make a start in creating a learning environment (not necessarily virtual) and 'getting the buggers to learn'!

Identifying key problems

Everyone is engaged in learning. They may not be learning what we want them to learn (so they may be away from *our* learning), but they are all learning.

(Rogers, 2003: 10)

It might seem odd to start the first chapter in a book about trying to get students to learn with an idea that everyone learns all the time. If that's the case, then what's the problem? If you accept Rogers' position, then the crux of the problem isn't about getting students to learn but rather about getting students to learn what you want them to learn: what's on the curriculum, what they need to be aware of to meet the criteria set, what they need to do to complete a project successfully or what they need to know to pass an examination. There may be a myriad of reasons why students are away from '*our* learning' but the first key problem to consider is that it's *our* agenda for learning, not necessarily theirs.

Adapting teaching to the needs of the student is a key driver in the 'personalization' agenda that is beginning to transform the FE sector (Hoare, 2007). The development of Virtual Learning Environments (VLEs) is not only for use as a teaching tool, but also as an administrative tool to enable a college to respond more effectively to the training requirements of employers, to streamline its admission procedures and to track students' progress, but it is also a way of making it possible for potential students to see what the college has on offer and for the college to record their interest and learn what their aspirations are. The significance of this development, according to Hoare, is a change of ethos in the FE sector: 'a willingness to listen to the students and respect what they do know', which allows students choice in the planning and recording of their own learning. In other words, there is a growing awareness that the learning needs of potential students are not neatly aligned to the college curriculum offer. The 'personalization' agenda is in its infancy and for many FE teachers a VLE is still a vision rather than a reality. However, acknowledging that students have their own learning agenda is something that everyone in the sector can take on board now.

The idea put forward by Rogers – that everyone is engaged in learning – is not a new one. Over the years there's been an idea that learning is like breathing or walking (Jarvis *et al.*, 1998; Visser, 2001) – you do it all the time and the majority of the time you're not aware of it. The analogy with breathing or walking implies that you do it without always knowing it and that you pick things up without always realizing that you are. Here are some examples which illustrate what these authors are talking about:

Experience	Learning from Experience
You appreciate how well you know your locality when a stranger asks for directions and you're able to give them without hesitating	You didn't realize you'd be able to remember so many street names and knew particular landmarks until someone asked you
You soon get the hang of changing nappies when you've got a newborn baby to look after	You didn't have any lessons – you just got on and did it and got better as the weeks went by
You learn the temperature control on your new cooker isn't exactly the same as on your old one when you've burnt the supper	You didn't deliberately burn the food but it wasn't until you had that you learnt about the difference in temperature control
Students lose interest in activities	You didn't set out to mess up the

you've spent ages planning and complain that they're too hard	lesson and only realized you'd pitched it too high when it went wrong
The weather forecast is 'good' but you grab an umbrella before you leave the house – just in case!	You learned you can't trust the weather forecast as you recently got drenched walking home from work when it rained unexpectedly

The examples above show that people are not necessarily aware of learning all the time and that it's sometimes unintentional. And it's the same for everyone.

That's a second key problem for teachers in FE: students don't always realize they learn 'naturally' all the time and often don't value what they have already achieved. Learning can happen at work or when you're enjoying your leisure time. Lots of learning takes place when you take on a new role such as becoming a parent or changing jobs. If you go on holiday abroad you are exposed to a different culture and become familiar with another way of life. You may even pick up a few words of a foreign language just by listening to staff when you order a drink or by checking the menu when you buy a meal!

If you start thinking about things you've learned recently, it soon becomes obvious that at times you may intentionally set out to learn something, such as how to say 'thank you' when you're in another country, but often you are probably just responding to the situation, such as the possibility of rain. Another interesting thing to observe is that learning can come out of both good and bad experiences. That's a relief to know as people often think all bad experiences are a barrier to learning. However, it's the experiences that life throws at you, whatever they may be, that provide the opportunity for you to learn.

Some of these experiences may be because you are living through a particular phase of your life or dealing with change and need different skills to cope with things. It is acknowledged that children are vulnerable and in need of particular support from teachers and others at times of transition and transfer, for example when moving to a new class or between educational institutions (Pollard, 2002), and this can apply to young people and adults as well. And that's just the sort of situation your students are in when they start on a new phase of their life at an FE college. Even if they're keen to succeed, students feel under pressure and wonder how they'll cope with attending college, learning a new subject or having a different teacher. An added pressure may be that they also go to school, work placement or employment for part of the week and have to deal with different rules, regulations and standards in those settings. Alternatively, they may be unemployed, at home with children, looking after relatives or recovering from illness and feel overwhelmed about coping with the hustle and bustle of college life. If they're not keen in the first place, for example they have a sense of failure or insecurity, then you've really got your work cut out to get them to learn *what you want them to learn*. How do you get their agenda and your agenda to coincide?

Although you may recruit and interview students individually and provide them with an Individual Learning Plan (ILP), the majority of students currently complete their college work in a group setting. You may be full of good intentions when you first encounter a new group of students, and convinced of responding to their needs, but when faced with a rowdy group or, perhaps even worse, a sea of sullen faces your good intentions begin to fade. Why won't they settle down to work? Why are they so disinterested in your sessions? You start to think about how you'll meet your targets and wonder whether you'll reach the figures for achievement. Without realizing it your agenda comes to the fore. Your priority becomes 'getting the buggers to learn'! Put simply, your energies go into getting them to learn what you want them to learn. It's your agenda – not theirs.

But, here's the crunch. A third problem is that you can't make anyone learn, you can't cause learning to happen. But it's not all doom and gloom: you can create conditions which give learning a chance! So why not make a start in resolving these key problems by thinking about using the way students learn 'naturally' and gradually build from that. You've got to start somewhere and a good place to start is the beginning – during interviews, taster sessions or induction. Everything doesn't have to be online for your college to be responsive to individual students' learning needs – it just requires a willingness to listen to students.

Talking about learning

All of us who teach in FE make assumptions about students on which decisions about planning sessions are based: what methods to use and what activities to choose. You can't help making assumptions because you can't know everything about every student who joins your group. However, if experiences are a rich resource for learning, as Knowles (1980) believed, then it helps to know more about what experiences learners have had. A good time to find out about how students learn 'naturally' is during an induction session. If your students have the language and ability to recall, then the following activity is worth a go. If your students are on a course for ESOL or for those with LDD then you will have to bring your imagination into play and adapt the activity to suit your particular needs.

Try this: Talking about learning

1) Ask students to think about what have they learned during the past year.
2) Use the information to develop understanding of the following:
    - What? Practice = New learning. Theory = Always learning.
    - How? Practice = Way of learning. Theory = Preferred approach.
    - Why? Practice = Wide experience. Theory = Social, cultural, work-related.

To start the activity suggested above, ask everyone to think about something they have learned during the last year and ask them to be prepared to share this information with others. Explain that it doesn't matter what it is, where they learned it or why – but obviously the example must be suitable for sharing with everyone in the group and not be offensive or embarrass anyone. If you can give them a fun example of your own learning, then this will really help.

Here are some examples that I've had from different groups of students which are not necessarily what you would expect and you will enjoy reading:

- 'I learned that if you put your car in reverse gear at traffic lights by mistake you go backwards and crash into the car behind.'
- 'When trying to paint a ceiling it's a good idea to wear something on your head, particularly if you've got thick, curly hair like me.'
- 'I learned I was expecting twins when I had a scan last week.'
- 'I learned a lot about global warming from watching a TV series, especially where a polar bear struggles to walk over melting ice. It made me think.'
- 'I learned that I was quite good at putting flat-pack furniture together and much better at it than my friend.'
- 'I learned that I could run for 3 km without stopping when I did a charity run at Easter – something I never dreamt I could do.'
- 'I learned that however hard you work at your job you can't avoid being made redundant if that's what the firm decides.'

You'll find that the request for learning experiences provides an opportunity for everyone to engage in conversation and it's a good icebreaker as well, because if you share a light-hearted example with the group to get them started this creates a relaxed atmosphere and each student can usually think of something to contribute without too much bother. However, the important thing is to:

1. Probe the shared experiences, and
2. Demonstrate to each student that learning has happened.

Let's see how you can develop the activity by asking the following questions: What? How? and Why?

- **What?**
  The exercise is an opportunity to build up a picture of each student and for everyone to get to know each other a little better. But the exercise is not just meant to encourage a nice, happy group feeling – that is only the start and it's much more than that. You use the students' examples to point out that *learning has taken place.* Make it explicit to everyone that they can learn and have proved it to themselves, you and each other. It's an opportunity for plenty of praise and a chance to encourage reflection on the fact that everyone in the group has learnt something recently and has a 'natural' ability to learn.
- **How?**
  You can discuss preferred ways of learning that have been exhibited by students by such observations and questions as:
    'You obviously like to be active.'
    'You sound like a practical, hands-on person.'
    'What is it about watching TV that helps you learn?'
    'Was it running with a group of others that spurred you to do more than you thought you could?'
  The responses to these observations and question can be used to reinforce the idea that everyone tends to have a preferred way of learning, but that people who learn best use a variety of ways and don't just stick to one preferred way. Many students will be aware of their learning styles from their school days or a previous college course and may be able to identify them. Some may be aware of the terms used in different inventories of learning styles and use them. If so, you must explain these terms to the rest of the group but don't dwell on them – it can become complicated and there's no real evidence that they have any educational benefits. It is generally better to refer to approaches to learning, or learning dispositions, using everyday vocabulary so that learning isn't seen as something separate from everyday life. Nevertheless, it's helpful to point out how different ways of learning can be

used in your subject and give examples because most students are interested in knowledge that is useful and immediately want to know how practical and relevant it is for them and how it will help them in what they're studying.
- **Why?**
It becomes clear that within one group there is a wide variety of experiences. Everyone chooses different examples of learning. Some are work-related, others connect to social roles, and there may be cultural reasons for learning. It's also important to stress that learning can be very rewarding (for example just think of the experience of a novice athlete completing a charity run), but it can also be tough – as learning about redundancy illustrates. Here you can introduce the idea that learning is an emotional business, and if a reason why students come to college is that they want to get the 'highs' that come with achieving their goal they need to be aware that they might have to go through the 'lows' to get there. And that's where you come in – so make sure you make it clear to the students that everyone experiences 'ups and downs' and you are there to support their learning and help them widen their experiences.

There has not been much research in FE colleges to evaluate the effectiveness of 'talking about learning' but a three-year project by Rudduck *et al.* (2005) that involved consulting school pupils about teaching and learning found that if their perspectives were taken seriously they felt more positive about themselves as learners. It was also found that pupils could understand and manage their own progress better and felt more included in the school activities. Knowing this, if college students believe what they say makes a difference then this is inevitably going to benefit FE teachers and help them understand how to support learning and build more collaborative relationships with students. Talking to students and the encouragement of 'student voice' is a key aspect of listening to the students' agenda – which supports personalized learning.

Minton (2005) also advises teachers to focus on students:

As teachers we can improve learning by bringing the process to the surface so that we can look at it. We can try to understand what is going on for the students and for us. We must try to see it, and feel it, from the students' point of view.

(Minton, 2005: 6)

The exercise outlined above in 'Try this' focuses on students: the discussion is about them, their examples, their experiences and their ways of learning. For that reason, it can be successful for any subject or level as the shared contributions come from the students and are not imposed on them. The significance of this is that it is *their* agenda.

Creating a learning environment

For many students, all too often the sessions at the beginning of a course become opportunities for completing administrative tasks, such as late enrolments, dealing with fees, sorting out timetables and rooms, or requests for student identity cards. The list is endless and can take up an inordinate amount of course time. What I am advancing in this chapter is an argument that initial sessions should focus on *learning* – not administration. Obviously you can't have students to teach without involving administration and they need to know administrative arrangements for their course, but it is all too easy for college systems to become a barrier to learning rather than a way of *overcoming* barriers to learning. A good FE teacher must focus on supporting the student in *learning* by creating the right conditions for this to happen.

Once you've shown that students learn unintentionally, it is time to move on and encourage them to think about how they can use their innate ability to learn *intentionally*. You need to explain the difference between the two: intentional learning needs to be *organized*.

Try this: Getting organized

GIVE students useful information
- Prepare a simple schedule/timetable template and ask students to enter details such as assignment deadlines, practical tests, assessment dates, examination times, visits, presentations, end of course, college closures.

GET students to think about how they might go about being organized
- Use the schedule and ask students to write in any dates they know about, such as work commitments, holidays booked.

USE the information to develop your students' understanding of the many things that need to be organized for learning to happen.

A practical and concrete exercise such as the one above raises students' awareness of how many things they have to take into account to be successful at organizing their learning. Students often have to book time off work, re-schedule shifts, arrange babysitters, organize lifts or work out bus or train timetables to attend college. Focusing on the idea that intentional learning involves preparation, such as getting to college on time, finding out about bus and train times, whether there is car parking available, etc., gives students the opportunity to plan ahead for themselves, organize their time, think about meal times and tell people what's happening. Cynics might say that this sounds very much like administration, but I would counter that by saying that is not the point of the exercise. The aim is to help students organize themselves for intentional learning.

Students' reasons for attending college and participating in your sessions are many, may be complex, or not really worked out, and significantly they are liable to change. If a student has clear goals – that's fine. However, if a student hasn't identified clear goals then asking them to specifically identify these introduces a source of

17

anxiety into the first session. Not all students are 'goal-orientated' and join a course for specific reasons with clear objectives; according to Houle's (1961) theory, some are 'activity-orientated' and join a course because they enjoy learning with others, or they may be 'learning-orientated' and join a course out of interest in the subject. I would, however, suggest that it is safe to take it for granted that students want to complete the course or qualification successfully (I don't think there can be many students who deliberately set out to be unsuccessful). Tell the students that this is *your* goal also as teacher, but that you can't achieve it unless they achieve their goal! Learning has to be a joint venture – a team approach. The purpose of the exercise, therefore, is to assist students in achieving their learning goals, that is, supporting the students' learning agenda and not that of the college administration. A constructive way of going about creating a learning environment is to focus on what students can do from 'Day 1, Week 1' to reach their goal. Avoid beginning by focusing on the distant goal; instead focus on the present things, people, time, activities, etc. by asking questions such as: When will you do your project work? How will you fit in reading and preparation? Where will you make space to do your college work at home? Who at home will help you be successful at college?

Focus on learning

At the end of the session it is a good idea to draw together the threads of discussion and convey the idea that there are not necessarily clear boundaries between different kinds of learning as the process involves a lot of things happening together. Students' discussion of their experiences, even if these seem a bit removed from your subject, is not irrelevant but provides an opportunity for sharing and exploring ideas about learning in general in relation to students' existing knowledge – which they need to bring to mind and be aware of to accommodate any new knowledge. If you make these connections explicitly in your responses and questions, then the exercises suggested in 'Try this' demonstrate that you are trying to get the students' learning agenda and your learning agenda to coincide. The dilemma of agenda-setting according to Richardson relates to:

> ... the dual and sometimes conflicting goals of introducing [students] to a particular content, and creating an empowering and emancipatory environment that requires that [students] own the content and process.
>
> (1992: 287)

Let's finish with a summary of ways to make agenda-setting empowering for students and to enable them to own the content and process of their learning.

Getting the buggers to learn: Focusing on learning

- Encourage students to talk about learning;
- Don't make assumptions about students in the group;
- Convey the idea that learning is 'natural';
- Find out as much as you can about how students learn 'naturally';
- Demonstrate it's possible to join in and enjoy a college session;
- Focus on students' learning and talk about what is required – explain, explain, explain;
- Remember that agenda-setting should be empowering and liberating for students and should enable them to own the content and process of their learning;
- Encourage the development of 'student voice' as a key aspect of personalized learning;
- Slow down – it's not about pushing and rushing at this stage but giving students time to absorb new information;
- Help students organize and manage the complexity of their lives as students, workers, partners, parents, family members, etc, so they can focus on learning;
- Be responsive, be patient – earn your money!

It is your actions that create a positive learning environment and in Chapter 2 you will be able to explore how these actions contribute to the conditions required for motivation.

2

WHAT ARE THE PROBLEMS IN GETTING STUDENTS MOTIVATED?

In this chapter you will find that some of the difficulties in getting students motivated to learn are because:

- Students may see their problems with learning as the responsibility of others;
- The way individual students identify their learning needs affects their motivation;
- Students' levels of motivation fluctuate;
- Students aren't interested or don't want to learn.

You will also find ideas for how to deal with these problems and how to help students recognize how they as individuals approach learning and what motivates them.

Different ways of seeing the world

The way we see the problem is the problem.
(Covey, 1989: 40)

If you see the problem of getting students motivated as a problem for you as an FE teacher to solve, then that might be the very problem! What Covey would say is that seeing the problem as yours only perpetuates the myth that the answer to problems is 'out there' and if only others would get their act together the problem would be solved. Perhaps you have heard students blame their lack of progress on others: *they* never encourage me; *they* don't have time for me; *they* don't offer to help; *they* just criticize me; *they* don't explain things properly; *they* go too fast; *they* go too slow; *they* just don't like me. The list could be endless and I expect some of these excuses have a familiar ring to them. When students complain like this it means that they tend to see the problem as outside their control: it is the fault of others and, therefore, they feel the remedy is in the hands of *others* – one of whom is probably you as their FE teacher.

Covey ingeniously describes this as an 'outside-in' way of seeing the world – that is, factors outside yourself such as other people's actions are the cause of your problems – and he

21

contends that this way of seeing the world does not lead to success in life. Whereas the people he studied for his research who were successful drew on characteristics inside themselves, for example, common sense and conscience, and they demonstrated what Covey termed an 'inside-out' way of seeing the world. To get many students motivated to be successful it seems you will have to convince them that the answer isn't necessarily in the hands of others and that they will have to make a shift in their thinking and come to accept that the answer is to be found *inside* them. This sounds like a tough proposition for you as an FE teacher to achieve – but in my view it is an even tougher one for the student.

Although I agree with Covey that success comes from within and that it is a result of an 'inside-out' way of seeing things, I don't agree that 'others' – the famous 'they' that students quote – can't *contribute* to your success. Just as with learning, you can't make anyone motivated if they don't want to be but I am convinced that 'outsiders', such as friends, family and teachers, make a huge difference and this chapter discusses how you as their FE teacher can help students deal with some of the problems they face in getting themselves motivated and develop a learning environment which encourages self-motivation.

The nature of motivation

Let's start by thinking about the nature of motivation itself. Essentially, it is about why people behave in a certain way, why they choose one course of action rather than another and why some continue along that course even in the face of problems whilst others give up. A student's motivation (in conjunction with their ability) influences their success in learning, whether it be passing an examination, meeting performance criteria or just persevering with college work. One of the difficulties for FE teachers is that motivation is unique to individuals and so a group of students will be motivated by many different things and these different things will motivate individuals to a greater or lesser extent.

In a similar vein to Covey's ideas about how we see the world, one classic way of looking at motivation is to see it as either extrinsic or intrinsic. If the things that motivate you are concerned with 'other things' or 'other people', that is, they are concerned with tangible things outside yourself, then this type of motivation is classified as extrinsic motivation:

- For some students, the thought of a pay rise keeps them motivated when studying for a qualification.
- For others, college is as much about meeting people and making friends as it is about getting down to some hard work.

Extrinsic motivation is related to what are seen as real rewards, such as increased pay rates, the possibility of promotion, enhanced status and forging social relationships.

In contrast, if the things that motivate you are concerned with 'personal things', that is, opportunities to use your own ability and gaining satisfaction from the nature of the task itself, then this type of motivation is classified as intrinsic motivation:

- Many students' motivation is related to a chance to make a better life and they thrive in rising to challenges in order to achieve.
- Many students are motivated by learning itself.

Intrinsic motivation is linked to opportunities to use your skills and knowledge and the satisfaction this brings. Intrinsic motivation increases with an appreciation of personal growth and development and is, therefore, primarily concerned with 'oneself' rather than others.

Motivation and learning needs

Maslow's (1968) theory about motivation, originally published as long ago as 1943, provides another way of looking at motivation. Maslow's research identified that people have needs, such as a need for food, safety, love, esteem, etc., but only *unsatisfied* needs motivate a person. If you don't have any food then you are motivated to go and find some. The theory is that there is a hierarchy or a series of levels of individual needs and it is only when people's basic needs for food, etc., are met that they are motivated by the needs at the next level, that is, safety, and so on. Although not designed with an educational context in mind, Maslow's needs hierarchy can be applied to students' learning as the following table demonstrates. Notice how learning needs change across the hierarchy.

Maslow's needs hierarchy	General rewards	Application to learning
1 Physiological	Food, water, sex, sleep	Refreshment facilities, pleasant conditions, reasonable workload
2 Safety	Safety, security, stability, protection	Well-planned timetables, student support systems, tutorial support, regular classes, order in class, safety around college
3 Social	Love, affection, belongingness	Opportunities for interaction, small group work, collaborative working, involvement in planning sessions, social activities, teacher approval
4 Esteem	Self-esteem, self-respect, prestige, status	Task differentiation, regular feedback, support for cultural values, formative assessment, peer learning/teaching, successful learning
5 Self-actualization	Growth, advancement, creativity	Self-directed projects, presentations, action learning, use of vocational/personal experience and skills, opportunities to be creative

(Adapted from Mullins, 1999, Table 12.2 Applying Maslow's need hierarchy, p. 419)

Many FE teachers don't question Maslow's needs hierarchy when they are introduced to it during their initial teacher training, and tend to accept the theory as it is usually represented in educational textbooks, that is, as a hierarchy at the peak of which is the achievement of self-actualization (which means you have realized all you are capable of becoming). This assumes that if students' basic needs are met then they will be motivated by their *unsatisfied* needs at the next level and thus will move one step nearer the peak of the symbolic triangle. It's as if you were a mountaineer; you struggle to climb the mountain stage by stage and battle with different conditions as you ascend and don't want the challenge to beat you, and it's only when you have set your flag firmly on the summit that you have a real sense of satisfaction. Not every mountaineer reaches the summit though, and may stop, give up or turn back at different points. Despite this they may feel a sense of satisfaction from just taking part in the expedition. You need to know where your students are on their learning journey and how they view their progress. What you can do as an FE teacher is question where your students are on Maslow's needs hierarchy, and consider how the 'Application to learning' column in the above table matches the way they are applying themselves.

A task for you as an FE teacher is to help students identify what their learning needs are. The problem is that if you ask them at the beginning of your course or programme, they probably won't be able to do this accurately. Further, if you know little about your students' needs, you might pitch your sessions too high and it may be too risky for students to admit they don't know something and so they won't join in. If you pitch your sessions too low then your students are likely to find them boring and switch off or play up. Pitching sessions at the wrong level is de-motivating for students. But getting students motivated is always a challenge and takes knowledge of your subject, your students and plenty of skill to get it right. Perhaps you can adapt the activity below to suit your situation.

Try this: Getting motivated

Devise a checklist which is appropriate as an introduction to the topic you have selected to start your teaching. This could be ten items or artefacts that you think students will be familiar with, so they could be things they know through common sense/general knowledge/experience or have covered at a lower level, for example terms, names, dates, expressions, sequences, ingredients, concepts, vocabulary, authors, book titles, theories, formulae, procedures, quotations, photographs, pictures – whatever's appropriate to the subject and level – and use PowerPoint or the real thing.

1. Ask students to tick each item on the checklist that they recognize, i.e. have they seen/heard of it before – these will become the things they won't need to think about!
2. Get students to add up the ticks and put their score on the checklist.
3. Share results quickly and applaud scores – the scores should be high if you've picked items well as the task involves simply recognizing them.
4. Invite students to select just two items and think about/write down why they are on the list/what they MEAN. Everyone is likely to be able to do this for just two items.
5. Share results quickly – students should all be able to contribute something and get confirmation that they're right, and also revise/review meanings of items they didn't pick.
6. Invite students to group together items that make sense – again all should be able to have a go at this as they've just heard meanings when sharing results.
7. Share results again – encourage plenty of discussion, give plenty of praise.
8. Now make links to new material/information.

The above activity provides an opportunity for students to experience factors that promote motivation, such as:

- A series of short activities rather than one long one;
- Receiving feedback as quickly as possible;
- Having knowledge of their success immediately;
- Using their previous experience and prior knowledge individually and collaboratively;
- Sharing positive experiences and doing well in front of their peer group.

You generally know whether you've pitched the activity correctly after the first minute; this gives you the flexibility to adjust the pace and feedback appropriately. For some students, just being able to tick a right answer is a new experience, together with there being no need to hide what they don't know. The secret is to keep praising and move on to the next step so that the pace is stimulating.

The activity also provides an opportunity for you as teacher to:

- Demonstrate that learning can be enjoyable;
- Identify what students understand and what they don't, and so identify appropriate support for their learning needs;
- Make explicit connections to new information and demonstrate your enthusiasm for the topic;
- Get students to think about, evaluate and analyse subject information from the outset in a relaxed manner.

All these factors create an environment in which students enjoy learning and experience success. Short, simple activities at the start of a programme give students the idea that success is attainable; a connection is made between existing skills and knowledge, and new learning. The extrinsic motivation provided by you as a teacher in the classroom is likely to increase students' motivation at the start of your sessions.

If the activity I've suggested doesn't seem right for your subject or level of students, it's well worth developing some short, simple activities of your own – they provide the extrinsic motivation that students seem to need most at the beginning of any new course or programme. (The example provided works at the beginning of any session.)

Ups and downs of motivation

Maslow did make it clear that the 'needs hierarchy' is not necessarily in a fixed order; he suggested that a good way to think of it would be as more of a continuum, and that needs can range from basic to higher level as circumstances change. The table adapted from Mullins (1999) above clearly depicts that, when the theory is applied to learning, students' needs change within the hierarchy. If you accept Maslow's contention that a continuum is a truer representation of motivation, then you must also accept that students not only progress up the hierarchy but also can regress down it. The case study below of a student doing an HE qualification in an FE college illustrates how motivation changes and was recounted to me by one of my colleagues. As you read it, see if you can visualize how it might apply to your subject and your students.

A case of fluctuating motivation

A confident and talented student had discussed his choice of project for an HE assignment with me in a tutorial and had begun planning the presentation and written paper. Some weeks later, and out of the blue, he declared that he had changed his mind about the topic he'd selected as he'd now got a much better idea. He realized just before the deadline for submission that he hadn't given himself enough time to plan, research and complete the assignment to the standard he wanted and so applied for an extension of the submission date because he had misjudged the time needed for his work. This request was turned down by the course tutor as it was not one of the criteria for granting an extension. The student was devastated but did manage to submit his work by the deadline, although he knew that it was not up to his usual high standard. For the next week or so I was plied with emails wanting reassurance that the work was OK. In one email he said he was hoping that I wouldn't think too badly of him, and saying how stupid he'd been to dismiss my advice and change his mind so suddenly and to not give himself enough time to

---

complete successfully. Another email arrived in which he said he wasn't cut out for studying and would pack it all in – he wasn't treated fairly in his request for more time and he'd never get the qualification he wanted now. After a flurry of emails on similar lines, I invited the student for a face-to-face tutorial as I have found that a student's poor performance and consequent despondency often mask personal problems they're reluctant to talk about. When he arrived we chatted for only a short time and he then asked for details about the next module so he could get ahead with the reading as he had learnt his lesson and wasn't going to go through that experience again! (Lecturer in Education Studies)

The above case study reveals that an individual's motivation fluctuates wildly. One minute the student is frustrated with himself and regrets his impulsiveness; the next he becomes aggressive and puts the blame on the course tutor. He then threatens to withdraw from the course and becomes fixated with the idea that he's a complete failure and resigned to not getting the qualification.

Maslow identified three classes of needs: primary (food, sleep, shelter); emotional (love, security) and social (acceptance by peers), which are all reflected in the case study above, and if we apply Maslow's theory as depicted in the table, the student moves from being self-directed (No. 5) to needing instant feedback (No. 4) and support from his tutor (No. 2). Finally, he moves back to self-direction and draws on his recent experience (No. 5). The student's motivation appears to be on a rollercoaster rather than a continuum!

The student's frustration and aggression are played out in the writing of emails as his motivation fluctuates, but could just as well have emerged in a class or a tutorial. If these emotions are recognized by the FE teacher then a brief, supportive response will be seen as appropriate – rather than an aggressive retort throwing back the blame and responsibility squarely to the student using words such as: 'You've only got yourself to blame. I did advise you against it'. The merging of theory and practice by the FE teacher, through support provided because of an understanding of the way motivation can fluctuate, eventually results in the student coming up with a way of solving the problem for himself by temporarily compromising his standards and accepting his circumstances – a positive outcome which you could easily apply to your students and your subject. The case study shows that what students want to achieve is their personal decision and often depends on how they feel and think about themselves and their circumstances at a particular time.

> **The effects of assessment practices on [students'] motivation and self esteem need to be continually borne in mind.**
> (Pollard, 2002: 310)

As the case study above shows, a teacher's support in a crisis is important as although it is recognized that failing can motivate a student to improve, this only happens if they have faith in their ability to succeed eventually.

Motivation and the individual

Motivation is plainly linked to the situation you find yourself in. An approach that might help you in solving the problems in getting some students motivated is to be found in Ecclestone's (2002) discussion of motivation and assessment. She relates how some people are 'embedded' in the educational system and, therefore, see education as a part of the process of 'becoming somebody' and as a natural development of previous experiences, say at home, in school or at work. You may know such people as they are characterized by having a good relationship with teachers and peers and enjoy everything that goes with being a student. They have a vested interest in doing well at college and getting their qualifications as their sense of self is linked with doing well in their chosen subject(s). It is their belief that attending college and gaining qualifications will 'open doors' for them and lead to future success and that's what keeps them motivated.

Here you can see that Ecclestone's argument that presenting motivation as *either* extrinsic or intrinsic is not helpful. From the above example of the 'embedded' student, it is clear that both extrinsic and intrinsic factors can motivate students. If a student puts in effort to achieve a qualification and they subsequently get that qualification then that is rewarding and fulfilling and encourages them to continue making an effort. It is evident to the student that effort is worthwhile and rewarded: it is both personally satisfying (an intrinsic motivator) and tangible (an extrinsic motivator). If such students are faced with difficulties at work or in their family life their motivation may waver, but they can usually get over the problems by making special arrangements to complete college work or by altering their immediate goal slightly until things improve. The determination to deal with the difficulties and remove the barrier to their learning – whether it is a personal problem, a stressful job, having to work overtime, looking after a sick relative or moving house – is spurred on by the knowledge that success is possible.

Conversely, another student may not be able to overcome very similar difficulties and might fail to complete assignments or keep up their attendance and drop out of college. It seems as if their motivation is not as strong and they see similar difficulties as insurmountable. Just stop and think for a minute why there should be such a difference between students and why there may be problems in getting some students motivated. Recent research with post-16 learners reported by Ecclestone (2002) reveals that students have very different dispositions to learning. For one group of young people education is just 'something to be got through' and what motivates many students is 'pragmatic acceptance'. In other words, the need to gain a qualification is accepted – but perhaps not with much enthusiasm. You would probably like to see your classes full of students who are highly motivated and perhaps your ideal students would be typified by the characteristics of students described as 'embedded' in the system, yet the reality is that most of them will be attending college because they have to be there if they want to get a qualification.

Often the problem with students' lack of enthusiasm can be

31

overcome by encouraging words of a *practical* nature which not only make explicit the connection between classroom activities and achievement of the qualification, but also provide praise for anything that will accomplish this. The following examples are worth a try.

Try this: Practical feedback and praise

- 'This is really useful – it's a topic that always comes up in tests.'
- 'This is needed to pass the exam.'
- 'This skill is really worth practising as you need it to get your qualification.'
- 'That's a brilliant result because these marks contribute to the final grade.'
- 'That's turned out really well. It's just the standard employers are looking for.'
- 'Everything's completed and cleared away on time – that's what customers will appreciate.'
- 'That's a good way to tackle the problem – what a good idea!'
- 'All the elements come together – it's a very creative approach.'

Practical feedback makes reference to what students know or have done and demonstrates the connection to the qualification or examination they are working towards. Praise for relevant but routine accomplishments highlights how short-term goals feed into long-term goals.

Whether you like it or not, and whether you might consider that making assumptions about transfer of learning is problematic, focusing on the relevance of classroom activities to achieving a qualification appeals to many learners who probably judge the quality of your sessions by their *usefulness* to their personal circumstances.

Providing extrinsic motivation

Getting students, whose one focus is getting the qualification, to engage in activities in class that broaden their experience but which they don't consider relevant to the qualification can be hard work. However, you can usually motivate students whose attitude is one of 'pragmatic acceptance' by acknowledging their attitude to learning and focusing your encouragement on their need to get a qualification, as the above examples in 'Try this' demonstrate. But how do you deal with those learners referred to in the reported research as 'hangers on', that is, those reluctantly in education and vulnerable to sudden disruption of this choice, or 'drifters' who are putting off life decisions because they are uncertain about what they want to do and not only lack direction but also lack self-esteem? You can identify so-called 'hangers on' and 'drifters' from questions such as:

- 'Why are you making me do this?'
- 'What's the point of it all?'
- 'Do I have to?'
- 'Why are we spending time on this?'
- 'Why bother?'

Responding directly to students' questions with logical reasons doesn't work. The conventional answer to these questions is that teachers are urged to meet the individual needs of students but this overlooks the power of *social* motivation and commitment to friends, peer groups or community. Trying to motivate individual students who have had bad experiences of schooling and negative attitudes towards education, to achieve a vocational qualification or improve their literacy and numeracy skills because this is what employers want is not easy when the students' experience tells them that there are few opportunities for full-time jobs and only low wages for what is on offer. Students' behaviour is shaped by their experiences and environment and they learn what is considered an acceptable way to learn, live and work (or not work) from their family and neighbours. It is idealistic to appeal to their intrinsic motivation, and to try to get them to identify their goals, etc., underestimates the power of their peers and family attitudes.

A more realistic approach would be to acknowledge that there are factors over which they have little influence and you and the college cannot readily change, but that there *are* things that you and they can control and change if they choose. My experience suggests that you must accept that motivation is affected by personal circumstances, but you don't have to accept that these necessarily determine motivation.

Focus on success

One thing that might get those students who perceive that the education system sees them as failures to think differently about themselves as learners is to create opportunities for them to be successful. If students lack intrinsic motivation then your primary task as their FE teacher is to provide extrinsic motivation.

Let's finish this chapter with a summary of ways to develop the learning environment to encourage self-motivation.

Getting the buggers to learn: Focusing on success

- Praise motivates, so use it to help identify the standards you expect in class;
- Avoid constant criticism, nagging, checking and calling out – it wears you out and really de-motivates the students;
- Support students through a crisis so they don't keep on failing and become de-motivated – help them to envisage success in the future;
- Make explicit how classroom activities link to long-term aims – help to keep students' dreams alive;
- Be prepared to provide extrinsic motivation – it encourages self-motivation;
- It takes experience to get the right balance between challenging students and spoon-feeding them – so keep working on this to be successful;

- Plan for successful learning through a series of short activities
  – success is an excellent motivator.

I hope you now agree that motivation is crucial for success in learning but that it is difficult to maintain even for the very keen students in a classroom or workshop that is unorganized, messy, hectic and unruly. In Chapter 3 I take a look at how the college environment contributes to, or diminishes, your endeavours in 'getting the buggers to learn'.

3

WHAT ARE THE PROBLEMS IN CREATING A LEARNING ENVIRONMENT?

In this chapter you will find that creating a learning environment is a problem because:

- The college environment is not always student-friendly;
- It is not recognized that physical facilities are external factors that affect students' learning;
- The impression created by a classroom is not generally evaluated;
- Organizational constraints are often not obvious;
- Poor relationships amongst colleagues can affect the atmosphere in the classroom;
- Classroom organization and management are only successful if underpinned by personal and professional values.

You will also find ideas about how to deal with these problems and how to overcome organizational problems that impede your efforts in 'getting the buggers to learn'. Further, you will be introduced to the idea of a 'holding environment' which both supports and challenges students.

Looking at the college environment

... one way to recognize why people behave as they do at work is to view an organization as an iceberg. What sinks ships isn't always what sailors can see, but what they can't see.
(Hellriegel, Slocum and Woodham, in Mullins, 1999: 17)

I know that global warming is linked to a changing climate and there is evidence that the polar icecaps are melting and great chunks of ice are breaking off and floating in the ocean, so just for a moment suspend belief and imagine that your college is one of these icebergs! One-third of it is above the waterline and visible but two-thirds are unseen, below the water. If you apply Hellriegel *et al.*'s theory to your college as an organization, then perhaps it isn't just the things that a visitor to the college campus can see that might be problems in creating a learning environment for students, but it is also the things going on below the surface, which they can't see. These unseen factors are just as likely to be the cause of problems that create barriers to students' learning, simply because they are hidden from public view and consequently they are not easy to deal with.

It's probably quite difficult not only to imagine your college as an iceberg but also to see it through an outsider's eyes. As FE teachers you become part of the college because you live in its organizational world and inevitably your organization has an impact on the way you work and behave. To help your students learn, you need to understand how the college functions and influences your behaviour. For a start, imagine yourself coming to the college for the very first time. What do you begin to notice? Of course, the building (or buildings) would be the first thing. So look around for the answers to the following questions:

- Is the college easy to reach by public transport?
- Is the signposting clear so facilities are easy to find?
- Is the building welcoming and accessible to all?
- Is parking and wheelchair access available?
- Is the reception area or information centre easy to locate?
- Is the learning resources centre, or student services facility, prominently sited?
- Is there evidence of up-to-date technology being used?

All these questions concern the things that can be seen, and you should be able to judge from them whether your college is a student-friendly place where students' learning is supported and where students really want to be.

If you've visited many FE colleges you know that both the location and style of buildings can vary considerably. Of course, college managers inherit buildings that were designed for a different age and funding regimes mean that finances are not boundless, but decisions about the way that money is spent on buildings and facilities can be seen as much more than simply technical or practical ones, that is, a means for achieving ends. There is a view that the culture of a college is manifest in its physical facilities, and according to Simkins (1998) the patterns and processes of resource management have *symbolic* implications, reflecting those things which are valued in the organization.

Good indicators of the organization's values that you should look out for are not only the state of the building and the use of technology, but also such things as the way rules and regulations are made explicit and the way students are regarded. Have another look around your college and note what you see, for example, corridors plastered with notices telling students:

- No Sitting Allowed
- No Eating or Drinking
- Photocopier and Computer for Staff Use Only
- Parking for Staff – No Entry for Students
- Office Closed – No Student Enquiries 12–2
- Staff Only – Students Please Use Side Entrance

If you saw notices like this you'd agree that they hardly reflect a student-friendly environment. Perhaps you can see that in your college students are considered differently and treated as valued customers and there is evidence of well-maintained premises, attractively decorated public areas, pleasant refreshments amenities, and adequate study areas and sports facilities.

You can make up your own mind about the messages the physical facilities in your college portray – and there may be conflicting messages to explain. But why is all this important and how is it relevant to students' learning? Creating a learning environment begins with the buildings because you must get students through the door and keep them coming back for more. Initial impressions do matter: what you can see above the 'waterline' reveals a lot!

Evaluating your teaching area

You may not have much control over central facilities, but what about your classroom or workshop – it is an integral part of the organization. Next time you've got a few seconds to yourself during a session, just stop and take a look around your teaching area – what does it tell you about your college as an education and training provider and about you as an FE teacher? Have you created the sort of environment that will motivate students and get the buggers to learn?

Imagine that an outsider has come into your teaching area. They could be an Ofsted inspector, an external examiner or a local employer. What sort of impression do you think they would get?

- Would the Ofsted inspector observe evidence of students' learning?
- Would the external examiner be able to ascertain that students were developing new skills through the curriculum?
- Would the employer see current practices being used and students making the most of up-to-date equipment/facilities or engaged in appropriate activities?

Put yourself in the shoes of these outsiders for a minute. What can they see? They are all looking for similar things: is the students' experience educationally, vocationally and personally worthwhile? Some of the questions that will be on their mind as they visit your teaching area will be:

- Is what is happening in the classroom personally meaningful?
- Is the college experience educationally enriching and pertinent to future study?
- Is the classroom activity vocationally relevant to employment?

Only you can say whether the visitors would be likely to provide positive answers to these questions. Only you can answer whether you would be happy for an outsider to visit your classroom without any warning at any time, any day of the week. I suspect not all FE teachers would be able to say an unequivocal 'yes' – myself included! You have to question whether it is possible to be a model of good practice all the time. You have to take into consideration the constraints to your professional practice, such as what it is possible to do in the classroom or workshop with the mix of students in the group, the numbers enrolled, possibly limited resources, student attendance linked to payment of grants, and the qualifications framework. You have to come to terms with these possible constraints; you have to juggle priorities and manage the classroom situation.

The realities of the classroom also reflect those things that are valued in the organization – such as the way resources are managed, as referred to by Simkins (1998) – and likewise manifest the culture of the college. Just as an FE teacher can provide extrinsic motivation to students (see Chapter 2), in a similar way the college environment and physical facilities are external factors that affect students' learning. The way physical facilities are arranged and organized has a direct influence on the classroom as a learning environment and the way it is arranged can have a significant impact on the quality of teaching and learning. Use the checklist below to see how your classroom/ teaching area fares.

Try this: Evaluating the teaching area

1. Give each item a score out of five according to whether it's 'not possible' (1) or 'just right' (5) by ticking the appropriate column.
2. Total your score for each section then add the scores together.

		Not possible			Just right	
		1	2	3	4	5
ENOUGH SPACE	To arrange desks/equipment as you see fit					
	To change the layout for different activities without major disruption					
	To all work comfortably and shift between individual or group work					
	To move around safely					

		1	2	3	4	5

ADEQUATE RESOURCES	To allow all students to undertake activities at the same time
	To give students practical experience of appropriate equipment, ICT, etc.
	To cover all parts of the curriculum
	To provide a variety of experiences
CONVENIENT CONTROLS	To allow blinds to open and close so students have enough light to work
	To keep the room warm in cold weather
	To keep the room cool in hot weather
	To allow students fresh air
ADEQUATE MAINTENANCE	To provide a clean and healthy place to work
	To show the room is cared-for
	To make sure all breakages are repaired
	To ensure all unwanted resources are removed and not stacked in a corner
ENOUGH ORGANIZATION	To keep records/resources available for use
	To allow for attractive displays
	To enable students to be proud of their specialist area
	To keep the space tidy and clutter-free

POSSIBLE SCORE = 100 ACTUAL SCORE =

3. Now you know how you rated your classroom, what about getting students to complete the checklist and then compare scores.

How did your teaching area score? What factors scored best and what factors scored worst? Was everything 'just right' and 100 per cent? The scores from the checklists completed by students would provide good information to include in a course evaluation.

Bear in mind that there is probably no perfect environment. Below is an example of what one FE teacher did, given the resources available at the time.

A case of making the best of things

I think a Business Studies classroom should be 'businesslike', like a modern office would be with plenty of storage, computer access and efficiently organized. When we recruited high numbers of students from school on vocational schemes we had to provide additional facilities really quickly – and these weren't really like a modern office. The room selected had old-style wooden office desks with three drawers on one side. We decided to call these 'workstations' and we set them out in two columns, back-to-back so that the room didn't look like a classroom and the wiring was safe. Then we numbered each one and put a chart of the room layout on the wall. The vocational students put their name against a particular number (as did all users of the room) and this was their 'workstation' for the duration of their course. We labelled the drawers and kept self-study guides for word processing in one of these; we put set textbooks in another; and examples of projects and a completed portfolio in the third one. Not only were the self-study guides, textbooks and exemplars readily accessible as resources for lessons but also, surprisingly, they did not go missing. The students were encouraged to take ownership of their workstations and to keep them organized as if they were in an office. I think this simple plan worked because the college classroom was not managed like a school classroom and the way it was arranged gave students a sense of what it was like to be in an office. It was a bit of a compromise until we got the funding through but it turned out to be a good 'bridging' experience for them between the workplace and school and a chance to learn about office procedures in a practical way. (Lecturer in Business Studies)

The case study above is a good example of the importance of physical facilities on learning and how adapting the classroom contributes to a learning environment. The organization of the room reinforced the idea that the students were adults and working in a 'businesslike' environment rather than a school, and for the teachers this was practical to maintain. The resources were stored safely and labelled clearly and they were openly available to students; they didn't have to wait for books to be handed out, or have to ask for them. Organization such as this influences behaviour, for example, students don't have to shout to someone on the other side of the room to pass them a book, or throw books across the room! Classroom organization does not have to be rigid – but can avoid time wasted on 'housekeeping' and disciplining students which can then be spent on teaching and learning.

Creating an environment for a purpose

What is 'just right' for one subject or FE teacher may be wrong for another. For example, the last thing a workshop for visual arts might need to be is organized with everything stored away neatly. An FE teacher in that subject area might want artefacts and materials around to provoke ideas and the keynote of such a classroom would be flexibility and creativity rather than organization and efficiency. The arrangement of physical facilities should reinforce the overall purpose of the teaching area. How does your classroom demonstrate your purposes and your curriculum aims and objectives? What would you reorganize if you could?

Whatever the subject you teach, physical facilities are crucial and if students can't concentrate – or don't want to work – they pick on the conditions within the classroom as a reason, as the examples below illustrate:

- 'It's too hot to work in here. I'm not doing any more. Can we go outside?'
- 'I can't concentrate because it's too noisy. Can I go to the library?'
- 'I'm going home because it's too cold to work in here.'
- 'This chair's too low. I can't see the screen. I give up.'
- 'I haven't got room to work – this place is rubbish!'

Before you can expect students to get down to learning you have to try to provide the right conditions for them. This often requires negotiating with managers and caretakers, which a lot of FE teachers resent because it takes up precious time, but the important things to remember if you do get involved in negotiations about heating and lighting, etc., is that you are doing so because improvements will benefit your students' learning. If you've been teaching even for a very short time, you'll be aware how disruptive room changes without warning can be, or a change of teacher at a moment's notice, or even worse classes cancelled or merged. When you have a group of students who've received news of room or staff changes, you'll have first-hand experience of the problems lack of continuity in the learning environment creates.

A good way of creating a learning environment is to encourage students to take ownership of an area – just as the Business Studies students who were the subject of the case study were encouraged to do. If students feel an attachment to their specialist area or subject room then they are more likely to take pride in it and feel part of the college community. The following are all examples of how students studying different subjects made their area of the college their own:

- Early Years – students painted self-portraits and displayed them in the classroom.
- Travel and Tourism – students put up photographs of their group on a study trip abroad.
- Sports Science – students took photographs of teams in their different kit and made a collage for display.
- Education Studies – students put up photographs of their graduation ceremony on the notice board.
- Art and Design – students organized an exhibition of their work around the college and in the grounds.
- LDD – students arranged plants that they had grown themselves in the greenhouse in their reception area.
- ESOL – students wrote stories about their background and home country and illustrated these with photographs, sketches and postcards and displayed them on the classroom wall.

A specialist teaching area that is aesthetically pleasing should motivate students. If students are encouraged to personalize their teaching area and FE teachers adapt physical facilities to the demands of their subject, then the foundations of a learning environment are created.

Hidden constraints

What outsiders or visitors to the college, such as Ofsted inspectors, external examiners or employers, will see when they visit your classroom are all observable or overt facilities, skills and competencies. But what about the aspects that the visitor cannot observe: covert and informal processes and behaviour? For example, when you know that an important visitor is expected do you have to make special arrangements to impress them? Do you have to change what you normally do or reorganize things and make special plans? Do you have to threaten the students or bribe them to behave for the duration of the visit? These may be short-term solutions to get you through a visit or an observation as on the surface everything seems fine, but they will not benefit anyone in the long run.

As a professional you are frequently faced with personal dilemmas about workplace practices and the way that you respond to them or resolve them reflects your own values. You may be pressed to take shortcuts in your preparations, make compromises in your teaching, be caught up with cover-ups about attendance figures or get into disagreements about marking. It's through the way you overcome these conflicts and disputes that you reveal your values. These underlying pressures arise through informal meetings or discussions which might take place in your curriculum team, and are often the result of personality clashes and differing attitudes. Everyone responds to such situations individually and as a professional you can make your own judgements. You don't have to take shortcuts that affect students' learning, you can discuss disagreements and thrash out conflicts and not participate in cover-ups.

A visitor to the college is probably unaware of your

professional dilemmas as you are being observed in the class-room. But remember, what sinks ships isn't always what can be seen, but what cannot be seen. If you want to create a learning environment you have also got to focus on solving problems caused by factors others cannot see. What you really need to think about is that it is the attitudes and actions of individuals that contribute to students' learning – both in a positive and negative way. It's very easy to blame others, as students often do, but you need to focus on your own attitudes and actions and make your values explicit.

When you face professional dilemmas you are confronted with your own assumptions about what it is right (or wrong) to do. Teaching in FE is a complex business and there are always choices to be made when implementing new policies or adopting new practices. Sometimes these choices may be made by you on your own, but more often than not they require decisions to be made jointly by members of a curriculum team or department. It is perfectly proper to have reservations about the adoption of certain practices and to challenge the ideas underlying new policies, or question the criteria on which decisions are based. You can have doubts about the proposed action or feel confused about the correct way forward. However, in challenging new proposals do you:

- Resort to threats which result in heated arguments with team members?
- Use your strong personality to ride rough-shod over colleagues?
- Refuse to discuss matters rationally with your managers?
- Storm off in a huff if decisions don't go your way?
- Create rifts with team members?

I expect you recognize these types of behaviour in colleagues, but reflect on your own behaviour for a moment as the way you go about dealing with professional dilemmas can have a direct bearing on the students' learning environment. Maybe you are convinced that you are morally right – or maybe you are just being stubborn and clinging to comfortable ways of working.

Who is to say who is right or wrong? Even though disputes between colleagues usually happen in team meetings or in informal conversations in the staff-room or office, they don't necessarily remain private and hidden from students. Disagreements between colleagues have an impact on students' learning because:

- Teachers are stressed about the disagreements and can't focus on the lesson;
- They are often discussed with students who may be urged to take sides or made to feel like 'piggy-in-the-middle';
- Decisions don't get made in time to implement changes that might benefit students;
- A bad atmosphere develops if teachers take out their frustrations on students;
- A lack of communication between colleagues can mean students are not told essential information, for example, about assessment standards and deadlines.

If your personal values and organization's values are at odds with one another then frustration, and possibly conflict, is likely to result. Individual needs do need to be satisfied and organizational goals need to be achieved. The answer is not just to shut yourself off and decide to go it alone and do your own thing. It is possible for personal and organizational values to be compatible. Therefore, if you are serious about creating a learning environment for your students, you must consider what goes on outside the classroom. Resolving dilemmas is crucial.

Try this: Resolving workplace dilemmas

What would you do in the following situations?

1. A student asks you: 'Is it true that our Course Tutor is leaving? We heard a rumour that he'd had a bust up with the Principal.'
2. A student leaves you a message: 'Can you have a look at the attached work I've just got back from the last module because

---

I don't agree with the marks? What do you think I should have got?'
3. A student stops you in the corridor and says: 'I know that someone in the class copied an assignment word for word from one of last year's students and yet nobody seems to have noticed.'

Possible solutions:
1. Don't feed into gossip and rumours.
2. Don't undermine your colleagues. Encourage colleague and student to communicate directly.
3. This matter needs careful handling – perhaps suggest a meeting between the student, your manager and yourself to verify facts before action is taken.

Some dilemmas appear unsolvable and sometimes you have to make a compromise to achieve agreement with colleagues or students. The case study in this chapter 'A case of making the best of things' is a good example of this whereby the FE teachers compromise by using the facilities available (which were not ideal) creatively to develop the kind of classroom that supported their students learning. This illustrates what Elliott (1991) advocates: the teachers adopt an approach which he calls 'creative conformity'. Elliott suggests that there are ways to comply with new policies and strategies rather than reject them out of hand, and then implement them creatively in the classroom. In this way you can incorporate your personal values and create a positive learning environment – and still achieve the college targets. To identify whether 'creative conformity' is for you try the following activity.

Try this: Working ethically

Reflect on the following questions and try to come up with answers:

- What wouldn't you compromise on professionally?
- What are the most important things about your FE teaching that are worth upholding or fighting for?
- What ethical dilemmas have you encountered in the workplace?
- How do you deal with ethical issues such as racial or gender intolerance?

Focus on the environment

Both visible elements such as physical facilities and underlying elements such as the attitudes of staff are interdependent; both contribute to creating a learning environment. However, success only comes if your classroom organization and collaboration with colleagues reflect your overall purposes as an FE teacher:

> ... to succeed, classroom organization and management strategies must relate to values, aims, requirements and curriculum plans as a whole and also to practical circumstances.
> (Pollard, 2002: 217)

Although Pollard provides clear advice about creating a learning environment, (Drago-Severson 2004) suggests that we think of achieving this in terms of a 'holding environment'. Drago-Severson explains that this was a term originally coined by Winnicot in the 1960s to refer to the kinds of special relationships within the environment that are needed for an infant's development, and that Kegan adapted this idea to lifelong learning. She describes a good 'holding environment' as serving three functions:

1. It must 'hold well', that is, recognize and confirm who the person is and where they are at without frustration. 'Hold well' in this context means supporting and caring (as in holding up) and not confining someone.
2. It must 'let go', that is, let the person move beyond where

they're at so that they can grow and, again, not confine them but enable them to develop their independence.

3. It must 'stick around', that is, provide continuity, stability and availability to the person who is in the process of growing, and also support the person they have grown to become.

These are features that any teacher can aim to provide in their classroom. Although the third feature may be difficult to achieve in a short-course, training event or modular programme, the first two can provide both the support and challenge essential to create a good learning environment. It's easy to visualize a 'holding environment' in relation to infants. You carry an infant in your arms, then they struggle to free themselves and when you put them down they toddle around and probably fall over. When they tire they want you to pick them up and carry them again. What you are urged to do is to visualize how you can apply the notion of a 'holding environment' to young people and adults in your college.

Creating a learning environment is clearly not down to one thing, and there is no rulebook to tell you what to do and when. You will need to work out why you want to organize and manage your classroom in a certain way and take into account how and when you want to do it. You should develop an approach which allows you to work without frustrating students and without personal conflict or professional discord, and be in general agreement with colleagues and organizational targets. Let's finish this chapter with a summary of ways of doing this.

Getting the buggers to learn: Focusing on the environment

- A key role for an FE teacher is to create a learning environment, and you must not lose sight of this in the hurly-burly of college life.
- The classroom or workshop reflects the values of a larger environment and you must interact with that environment rather than work in professional isolation.

- Organizational policies and targets can be achieved through 'creative conformity' without discarding your personal values and ethics.
- The way classrooms are organized influences the behaviour of the students, style of teaching and can help facilitate students' learning.
- Encourage students to respect their environment and set a good example through the way you organize and treat the classroom.
- Respect students' commitment to the college course and keep them informed of impending changes so they have time to adjust.
- Remember that students talk to each other so avoid gossiping about colleagues with them and don't involve them in personal disputes.
- Contribute to collaborative decisions about students' learning by attending appropriate meetings and discussing issues professionally.
- Both supporting students and challenging them are features of a 'holding environment' and essential in creating a good learning environment.

4

WHY ARE THEORIES ABOUT STUDENTS' LEARNING CONSIDERED A PROBLEM?

In this chapter you will find that theories are often considered a problem rather than a help because:

- Theory and practice are thought of as opposites;
- Theories often seem to contradict one another;
- Theories go in an out of fashion;
- Some theories seem just like common sense;
- Theories don't appear to apply to your students, subject or qualification framework.

You will also find ideas about how theories help to explain how and why things happen as they do, and how useful they can be in helping you to understand the problems in 'getting the buggers to learn'.

Theorizing is something we all do

When used in daily discourse, the word 'theory' signals no magic powers. It awards no special status to an idea, any more than other everyday words like premise, hunch or conjecture. I have friends who tout a fanciful theory that Hollywood film stars always die in threes, a light-headed notion that proves accurate time and time again – provided, of course, that one is flexible about the counting.

(Wolcott, 2001: 80)

Wolcott points out that in everyday life we use theories all the time, but if I suggest to students undertaking their initial teacher education that theories are useful and invaluable for developing their practice in the FE sector, I am instantly aware of their raised eyebrows, watch their eyes roll skywards and can hear their groans of disbelief. I am dismissed as someone who doesn't really know what goes on in their classrooms today. I can almost hear them thinking: doesn't she realize that 'teaching is seen more and more as a practical activity in which experience is valued over theoretical knowledge' (Armitage *et al.*, 2003: 249).

I don't know about Hollywood stars but you must have all

heard of a similar theory that 'buses always come along in threes'; here, again, flexibility about the counting is needed! We are all theorists in a way because in our everyday life we develop hunches about things. If you don't subscribe to the theories about Hollywood stars or buses – what do you have a theory about? Of course, if you have a hunch it's probably guesswork, but it's based on observation which is a method a lot of researchers use. Your hunch probably contains a kernel of truth which offers an explanation of a situation that intrigues you but that you can't really explain.

However, if you try to link the word theory in the same sentence with teaching and learning in a session for trainee teachers, the usual response is scepticism. The word 'theory' seems to carry the magical powers that Wolcott mentions – it seems mysterious and complicated in trainee teachers' minds – and it takes on a special status. Any mention of theory seems to perpetuate the idea that theory and practice are at opposite ends of a spectrum. What is talked about in the education studies classroom doesn't seem to apply to the situations that trainee teachers find themselves facing in their own classroom: educational theory and classroom practice appear to be two separate things.

Whilst standing by my conviction about the usefulness of theory in a practical activity such as teaching, and that applying others' ideas helps you develop your practice, I accept that there are real problems for novice FE teachers surrounding the idea of assimilating educational theory – and I expect you have noticed how your own students switch off at any mention of work involving theory. These problems are addressed in this chapter with an aim to convince you that theory really does help in getting students to learn. Examples will be provided so you can judge for yourself.

Theory and practice

Let's first address the aforementioned problem of theory versus practice. The Oxford English Dictionary suggests one definition (among others) of theory as: 'department of art or technical subject concerned with knowledge of its principles or methods, as opposed to *practice'*. It seems that it is official: according to the dictionary, theory and practice are opposed to each other. So it's understandable that trainee teachers think of theory and practice as separate. But this oppositional view has a weakness in that it underestimates the extent to which those who teach have to reflect on what they are trying to do. When you reflect on what you are trying to do in the classroom as an FE teacher, you are in fact theorizing about your practice and trying to think of an explanation for what is happening (or has happened) and formulating a way to improve or do things differently in the future. According to Pollard:

> ... such theorizing is an integral part of reflective teaching because it represents an attempt to make sense of data and experience. It is an opportunity to develop creative insights and an occasion to consider any discrepancies between 'what is' and 'what ought to be'.
>
> (Pollard, 2002: 64)

In Pollard's view, practice is not opposed to theory as he identifies theorizing as an integral part of practice, and that those engaged in reflective teaching gain 'creative insights' from theorizing. In other words, classroom teaching involves the individual FE teacher taking action in a particular situation but – and this is important – this is guided by a set of beliefs about teaching, which can be developed through reflection. Hillier (2005) explains this well when she says:

> What, in fact, is happening is 'theory-guided practice' where what we do presupposes a conceptual framework, even if we are not terribly good at articulating it or even aware of it. However, we can, at times, decide to use theory to guide our practice.
>
> (Hillier, 2005: 10)

As an FE teacher you are guided by theory in the form of a conceptual framework, which is a set of beliefs which governs how you teach, even if it's implicit or unspoken and you're not really aware of it. This idea is supported by Gibson (1986) who says that theory and practice are indivisible as there is always a theory underlying and embedded in any practice. However, he contends that it is critical theory which offers ways that help teachers establish a *rational* justification for their practice (rather than reflection) and which enables teachers to place their own practice and experience at the centre of their professional development. Gibson states that the central intention of critical thinking is to gain knowledge and power and to be in control of one's own life – which could be considered as the purpose of education. So, it's also good to know that, as Hillier suggests, you can take the decision to use theory to guide your practice if you wish. I too would encourage this in all teachers who are seeking to develop and improve their practice.

There are some academics who suggest that practice is just *re-presented* as theory (Armitage *et al.*, 2003) when teachers begin to reflect and develop an explanation of their practice, and they see this reflection as an attack on academic knowledge. They challenge the idea that the restructuring of the teacher's own experience through reflection is theory (yet they do acknowledge that although this is not the traditional way of developing theory, it may help teachers in developing their practice). They contend that the theories developed in traditional ways through research and critical thinking provide an important framework for teachers through which to understand the wider educational environment – whether we need the theories for immediate practical use or not.

The theories that you might use to guide your practice are made up of general principles that are developed through research to help you make sense of what's going on. Theories are like sets of rules that connect ideas and explain the relationship between things. Behaviourist learning theories are good examples, dating back to early classic research studies carried out at the beginning of the twentieth century. Different principles of learning have been developed over time by different theorists. One of these principles was 'operant conditioning' which was identified by Skinner (Hicks, 1999), who demonstrated the relationship between 'a stimulus' and 'a response', which can be 'reinforced' by 'a reward'. Skinner's theory is that a response to a stimulus can be learned and to prove this he showed how an animal associated a response with a reward. Part of the research involved hungry rats in a cage, in which there was a lever (stimulus). The rats learned that pressing the lever (response) resulted in getting food (reward). The rats pressed the lever unintentionally at first but the 'conditioning' to press the lever took place because each time they did they got a reward (i.e. food), so the reward reinforced the response. Skinner then went on to discover that positive rewards worked better than negative ones – such as making the rats fearful – but what is really interesting is that he found that if the rats didn't always get the food when they pressed the lever, that is, when they were not rewarded *every* time, this strengthened the stimulus–response bond. Now that's something that you probably wouldn't have expected!

So, how can all this research on rats at the beginning of the last century be *useful* to you as an FE teacher at the beginning of the twenty-first century? Well, what you must do is apply the theory to your practice. For example, if you give a student a task (stimulus) and they complete it (response) you praise them or give them a high mark (reward). This then acts as reinforcement and the student is likely to persevere with other tasks. Students learn that completing college tasks successfully is the way to make progress. On the other hand, no praise or a poor mark would be negative reinforcement and the student is likely to give up or lose hope. However, if a student always receives the reward of praise or high marks then Skinner's theory would suggest that the reward is no longer reinforcement. Now, that's useful to know as you would naturally think that praise or high marks would always be effective, but if you always give them unthinkingly then the theory is that in fact what you do is lessen the value of praise or a high mark as a reward. A good example comes from a student in early years education who is the subject of the case study below, which seems to support Skinner's theory.

A case of diminishing returns

I got good marks in the first year of my course for all my assignments but I had the feeling I could do better but didn't really know how. In tutorials when I mentioned this, the response from several teachers was things like: 'Your work's fine', 'It's fine', 'You're doing fine, don't worry'. It was probably true but I was frustrated. I just felt I would like more of a challenge. Telling me everything was fine every time didn't help me or spur me on to do better in the second year.

Maybe you would have responded to the student like the tutors did in the case study above. However, once you've read the case study you can appreciate that praise by itself is not always enough to motivate students. Petty summarizes the student's reactions to feedback effectively when he says:

> They will hate being ignored; they will be encouraged by praise; and as long as their successes are recognized and praised, they will probably find any reasonable constructive criticism challenging rather than demotivating.
>
> (Petty, 2004: 64)

Having read about 'operant conditioning', did you recognize the allusion to this theory in Petty's advice? Perhaps it will make you think differently about how you provide feedback to a student and enable you to praise some aspects of their assignment by highlighting its strengths, to criticize other aspects which need development and to provide guidance about how to achieve a higher standard in the future. I hope this illustrates my point that the purpose of researchers and experts in developing theory is to provide general principles, methods or rules that can then be applied to problems in practice, helping *you* to make sense of what's going on. Knowing a theory can, therefore, be very useful as you can apply that knowledge to your practice to support students' learning. In this way you can not only appreciate, but also demonstrate, that theory and practice are not in opposition to each other.

Theories contradict each other

This brings me to my next point, which is the perennial complaint that theories seem to contradict each other and so are more confusing than helpful to an FE teacher. A good example of the contradiction that trainee teachers complain about is apparent in the difference between the behaviourist theories I've just discussed and humanist theories. The different roles identified for the teacher and student illustrate this point well.

- Behaviourist theories emphasize the role of the teacher. The teacher selects the task that is the stimuli and provides reinforcements by praising correct responses (or ignoring incorrect ones). The teacher is active as they deliver the session and pass on the subject knowledge or demonstrate a skill, and the student is comparatively passive as they sit and listen or watch and try to take it in. Although the student has to provide the responses it is the teacher who judges whether they are right or wrong and so the student is motivated by external rewards. Behaviourist theories dictate a step-by-step approach to learning, which has advantages in that topics are introduced in a logical order, but the teacher not only selects the subject content, organizes the activities and assesses the students' responses, but also paces the delivery of the session and in a class with mixed abilities this may not suit every student. Behaviourist theories require teacher direction and control.
- Humanist theories, in contrast, emphasize the role of the student. The student sets their own goals, and motivation for learning is regarded as coming from within. Rogers (1983) was a proponent of humanistic principles and considered the role of the teacher as an over-rated function. What Rogers considered important was for the teacher to help facilitate

students' learning as he contended that both the content of the learning and the process of the learning should be in the hands of the student. Humanistic theories require students to take full responsibility for their own learning, both what they learn and how they learn it.

It is evident from the brief descriptions above that there are contradictions between theories. When you are reflecting on your practice and trying to think of an explanation for what is happening, do you subscribe to one of these? Have a go at the following activity to find out.

Try this: Identifying personal theories

With your lesson plans in front of you, evaluate your last three sessions to uncover what theory (or theories) might be implicit within them.

- Do the plans indicate whole-class teaching or is there provision for individual and small-group work?
- How do the plans indicate ways to pitch your lesson appropriately for all learners?
- How do the plans involve the students in decisions about the session?
- How do the plans allow for you to assess whether students have found the instruction/new knowledge personally meaningful?
- How do the plans enable students to connect with their existing experiences and understanding?

When you have thought about the questions, evaluate what your answers tell you about your role as a teacher and the role your students take. Are contradictions revealed that need addressing? Consider whether your answers reflect one of the two theories discussed above more than the other. If there is a mix of both, then perhaps this is *your* theory about teaching! You may have developed the 'creative insights' that Pollard (2002) suggests come from such theorizing.

One of the reasons for the differences in approach discussed in the section above is that humanistic theories were developed as a reaction against behaviourist theories. Learning proved a demanding subject for research at the beginning of the last century as it is a complex process and involves the workings of the mind which are hidden from view, for example memory and intelligence were difficult to observe and measure. The view that emerged later on was that behaviourist theories were seen as reducing the special nature of the human being, as the research involved animals. The contradictions arise between the theories when theories are challenged by new ideas. If others challenge theories, then you can too. You don't have to accept what the theories say, but I would urge you to at least think about them and, like other theorists, have some of your own new ideas to put in their place before you reject them out of hand.

Theories go in and out of fashion

What's happening in the 'outside world' inevitably has an influence on what happens in the world of education. What is happening now, according to Jarvis (2002: 21), is that: 'Teaching is changing; it is being forced to change by the dominant globalizing forces of social change'. This change demands the introduction of a new curriculum for the FE sector as policy-makers finance – and employers demand – qualifications that are work-related, competence-based and which foster employability and citizenship. A changing world places pressure on the government to maintain competitiveness in the nation's trading and commercial activities in a global economy, and individuals have a vital role to play in society and in the economy. This role requires education and training because with changing technology non-skilled workers are not in demand but skilled workers are. As you might expect, this means that teaching methods, assessment and class organization in FE colleges begin to change and theories that were once relevant and pertinent to FE teaching become outmoded.

Learning is now at the heart of the government's educational agenda and is presented as the key to a strong economy and an inclusive society. Armitage *et al.* reveal how pervasive the term 'learning' is in educational policies:

> 'Learning' is the buzz-word of the new millennium – the 'learning age.'. We live in a 'learning society', where 'lifelong learning' has replaced a lifelong job; we work in 'learning organizations' and shop in the 'learning market' . . .
>
> (Armitage *et al*, 2003: 60)

As the years of the new millennium's first decade speed by (and may have since passed when you read this), learning is still at the forefront of current government policies – but this is now accompanied by 'vocationalism'. So what theories help you get students to learn at a time when society requires the delivery of a wholly vocational curriculum in FE colleges?

A theory of learning that takes into account knowledge derived from, and required to be part of, society, and which places the student in an active role in the process of learning is a social-constructivist theory of learning. The principles of this theory were developed through research into the interaction between people and their environment, and embrace the notion that learning takes place in a social context (Vygotsky, 1978). Although this approach to learning has been influential with children since its introduction over 30 years ago, it has not been widely adopted by FE teachers and is still a relatively new approach when teaching adults and young people. However, this theory is particularly useful in 'getting the buggers to learn' as it focuses on how teachers, or family members, work colleagues or peers, can support a student's learning – something that other theories often underestimate.

In a vocational classroom or workshop the FE teacher plays a key role as someone who is experienced in the craft or skill the student is attending college to learn. The teacher can draw on their considerable experience and use their skill to support students' learning. Social-constructivist theories focus on:

- students being active and discussing their learning with others;

- the significance of making sense of things with appropriate guidance;
- building on previous knowledge – perhaps acquired from home or the workplace;
- developing that knowledge through instruction and support from a more experienced person, i.e. through constructive intervention;
- scaffolding students' understanding/skills, i.e. helping and guiding them, until they can do things on their own.

The importance of these features for students is that they model the way learning takes place in childhood, that is, a more experienced person helps with a task or problem that the child can't complete on their own. According to the theory, this help takes place in the impressive-sounding 'Zone of Proximal Development' (ZPD). The zone, as defined by Vygotsky, is the distance between the actual level of competence of the student solving a problem on their own and the level of competence achieved with help and guidance from a teacher (or another person). A teacher's role is to support the student by instructing, questioning, prompting them to think, demonstrating, etc. so that they can do more than they could if they were left on their own to sort out the problem. Although social-constructivist theory models how learning can be supported in any social setting, for it to be successful in a formal setting such as a college requires considerable skill on the part of the FE teacher. If your students are reluctant learners, have had poor experiences at school and haven't developed the basic skills that you'd expect, then they might easily interpret any help as patronizing and demeaning to them. You convey this if you regard students as inadequate or lacking drive. You are likely to be more successful if you just think of students as less experienced simply because they've had less time to practise and gain experience and expertise than you have. In this way, what you are acknowledging is that students have *potential* to gain knowledge and skills – not that they are not capable.

I don't know if Vygotsky had the Latin phrase *'proxime accessit'* in mind when he was labelling his new concept 'zone of proximal development'. The Latin phrase literally translates as 'he came very near' and was used to describe the position of a person who is nearly equal to the actual winner of a prize or scholarship, that is, a runner-up. As a teacher, through your intervention, instruction and support in the 'zone of proximal development', you can enable runners-up to become winners!

Supporting students in realizing their latent potential and enabling them to see that they have in them the makings of a budding expert in a particular skill is as rewarding for the teacher as it is for the student. It was Bruner's (1990) research which labelled the process of developing potential as 'scaffolding'. Scaffolding students' learning means recognizing their promise and noting any aptitude in your subject and making it explicit to students that you will support them in what they want to achieve. With your support they can become part of the class as they engage in learning. It is then possible for them to see that they could become a member of a craft, trade or professional community in the future. You might encourage the runners-up to become winners – but don't expect to win round all of them – achievement does require real commitment from students and an intention to make the most of their own ability. It also requires a willingness to discuss their learning, and the social capability to envisage their future in their community. Here follows an activity that will help you develop an awareness of those students who might benefit from scaffolding.

Try this: Scaffolding to develop potential

Next time you set students individual tasks, pay particular attention to the variety of behaviours that indicate that a student could do with help, and which might in turn result in your providing a 'constructive intervention'. Are they:

- Sitting quietly and just staring out of the window?
- Pretending to get on, but looking around anxiously to see what everyone else is doing?
- Disturbing other students by messing around?

- Shouting out and demanding attention?

Which would be the most appropriate way of scaffolding a student in your subject, in your classroom?

- Watching?
- Listening?
- Demonstrating?
- Questioning?
- Collaborating with peers?
- Encouraging group discussion?

You can learn a lot by observing students before rushing in and helping. Just because a student is making a fuss and demanding attention, it doesn't mean they are the only one who needs 'scaffolding'. The answer is that *all* of your students will benefit from scaffolding and the way you do this requires a high level of judgement, knowledge and skill which comes with practice.

Theories are just common sense

You probably wouldn't have immediately realized what 'zone of proximal development' meant or what 'scaffolding' implied in relation to students' learning. However, once you have worked this out such theories might seem more like common sense than rocket science. This can apply to many theories, which are designed to explain things and to help you make sense of things. Theoretical models are particularly good examples as they tend to simplify the relationships between things – either visually or with the use of figurative language, for example, labels or metaphors.

Now, that you understand what the theories of 'zone of proximal development' and 'scaffolding' mean, you will want to apply them to practice. A way that you might achieve this is through assessment – but not the assessment which involves tests and exams. Instead think in terms of making a 'diagnostic appraisal'. Rowntree (1987) included this concept in his theoretical model 'Assessment, Evaluation, Diagnosis and Grading' over 20 years ago. At that time, his model was ground-breaking and within it assessment of students' learning was depicted as recurring throughout the process of teaching. From this assessment students' needs were diagnosed, and teaching effectiveness evaluated. Until the introduction of this model, an FE teacher's focus had been on summative assessment at the end of the course rather than on formative assessment which happens throughout learning. In Rowntree's model the ongoing assessments and consequent diagnosis are used to adjust the pace and content of teaching, and the series of assessments contribute to a final assessment and a grade.

The idea of the process of teaching and learning being modified by assessment has particular relevance today. Indeed, Jones (2005) promotes this idea as 'assessment for learning' and states that 'teachers make professional judgements on students' performance in every teaching and learning session undertaken, whether consciously or subconsciously'. The professional judgements referred to by Jones are in fact formative assessment and FE teachers are urged to use the information gained to identify particular learning needs and gaps in understanding. Effective FE teachers are aware of how they make and use these judgements, and their secret is that they reflect during lessons and become aware of what's going on, that is, make the judgements consciously rather than subconsciously.

The notion of formative assessment has rightly gained popularity recently, yet there is another theoretical model of assessment published by Earl in 2003, i.e. before Jones, that demonstrates how formative assessment, that is, assessment *for* learning, is just one approach to assessment. This theoretical model is depicted in the table below and should be considered in your quest for 'getting the buggers to learn'.

Notice the subtle use of language in Earl's model; it all hinges on three words '*of*', '*for*' and '*as*'. It's surprising what a difference such tiny words can make:

- Assessment *of* learning involves the teacher making judgements about the student's future based on what they have learnt.

Approach	Purpose	Reference points	Key assessor
Assessment of learning	Judgements about placement, promotion, credentials, etc.	Other students	Teacher
Assessment for learning	Information for teachers' instructional decisions	External standards or expectations	Teacher
Assessment as learning	Self-monitoring and self-correction or adjustment	Personal goals and external standards	Students

(Earl, 2003)

- Assessment *for* learning also involves the teacher making judgements which then assist them to modify the way they teach to help students learn.
- Assessment *as* learning identifies the student as the key assessor and the one who makes adjustments to enable them to achieve personal goals and qualifications.

The idea that I would like you to try out is the last one. If you combine the approach of 'assessment as learning' with 'scaffolding' you will encourage students to build on their experience and gradually construct knowledge and skills. Self-monitoring and self-correction will come through the initial interdependence of teacher and student. You will have to prepare students to become proficient at assessing their own learning achievements and gradually move to assessment *as* learning where the students become the key assessors of their own learning and development.

Try this: Using assessment as learning

1. Get students to informally assess themselves as students and identify the criteria they use for self-assessment.
2. Get students to examine how beneficial particular learning outcomes are to them in relation to their intended future employment.
3. Get students to produce a timetable or schedule to identify how much time they intend to invest in completing an assignment to meet the deadline.
4. Get students to provide a self-assessment of a completed assignment and then compare it to tutor feedback in a tutorial.

Theories don't apply to your context

Theories are *general* rules or principles that predict what is likely to happen – but only if the same conditions are present or the same relationships apply between the events or facts. This provides one explanation for why theories don't always appear to apply to your circumstances. Another reason might be that it takes professional experience to make the links and if you are just embarking on your career as an FE teacher you will not have had time to widen your experience of teaching and learning to enable you to make connections to the range of theories out there. A more significant reason why theories don't seem to apply to your subject, students or the qualifications they are studying for, is that not only are no two classrooms exactly the same, but also neither are students, as Eisner points out:

> ... education is a process whose features may change from individual to individual, context to context.
>
> (Eisner, 1985: 91)

Practical activities in each classroom come with distinctive and unique circumstances which one can never duplicate exactly, and it is impossible to predict the outcomes with complete assurance.

The following strategies are useful in taking the individual student's needs and context into account to contribute to a personalization agenda:

- Portfolio development;
- Workplace learning and assessment;
- Student choice of topic for assignments;
- Presentations by students in college about their workplace practices to share new ideas with their group and discuss similarities and differences in other workplace settings.

Focus on developing ideas

In this chapter I have encouraged FE teachers to think of theories as useful tools for thinking about students' learning. Further, I have shown that theorizing is an integral part of reflective practice and something that teachers do in their everyday life. Woods (1996) discusses the contention that the expertise of teachers comes from 'practical professionalism' which stems from intuition and experience rather than scholarly disciplinary knowledge. However, my response would be that you have to apply scholarly, disciplinary knowledge to practice to develop expertise, and my contention is that the more you expand your awareness of your own theories and understanding of and applying others' theories, the more expertise you will develop in 'getting the buggers to learn'!

Getting the buggers to learn: Focusing on developing ideas

- Theorizing is something we all do to arrive at explanations for what is happening in the classroom.
- Theorizing is integral to reflective practice as an FE teacher.
- Developing awareness of your own theories about teaching

and learning also reveals the values you hold about education.

- Applying others' theories to practice helps you improve your practice.
- Remember that others' theories might not fit your situation exactly and won't provide an instant solution to your problems.
- The nature of theories means that they can be disputed. You can challenge or reject others' theories, but it is good if you have your own ideas to put in their place.
- Keep up-to-date with new ideas and theories and be aware of 'what's in' and 'what's out' in FE teaching.
- Scaffolding and 'assessment *as* learning' are two common-sense theories for getting students to learn.

Chapter 5 looks to the problems with learning from the student's perspective, which is often at odds with the FE teacher's perspective.

5

WHAT ARE THE PROBLEMS WITH PROBLEMS WITH LEARNING FROM A STUDENT'S PERSPECTIVE?

In this chapter you will find that the problems students identify with learning are:

- Poor experiences in previous learning situations;
- Poor experiences on a current learning programme;
- Expectations of the learning programme are not met;
- Expectations of themselves as learners are not met.

You will also find ideas about how to deal with these problems, how to deal with emotional issues and how to see things from a student's perspective.

Perceptions differ

Teachers should be fair, with no teachers' pets, and no pet hates.

(Petty, 2004: 81)

This brief statement is described as 'studentese' by Petty and is a student's translation of the following 'teacher-speak': 'All students must feel that they are positively and equally valued and accepted'. Petty admits that few teachers intend to give what he terms 'unequal opportunities', but he asserts that most do. However, it is not just the difference in the use of language that is significant; what Petty highlights in this translation into 'studentese' is that teachers and students perceive things differently. For example, a teacher's behaviour towards a student may be considered by them as fair but be perceived as discrimination by the student (however unintentional this may be) and thus considered by the student as 'unfair'. The student's perception is that the teacher thinks of them differently and treats them differently. The teacher is probably not aware of this immediately or directly as it will only be communicated through the student's subsequent behaviour towards them.

What the statement in 'studentese' communicates clearly though is that if you want to find ways of 'getting the buggers to learn' you have to be aware that, although teaching is a two-way process, Petty suggests that as a teacher you have no direct control over the students' learning as the students form their own perception of the process. They have their own ideas about what teachers and teaching should be like. To support this idea, Petty (2004: 78) draws on Carl Rogers' view that: 'It is perception not reality which is crucial in determining behaviour'. If you take this on board, it means that if you have a class of 20 students there will be 20 different perceptions of reality – or rather 21 as you will have your own! Rather than leaving things to chance as you have to in a game of cards, the intention of this chapter is to present a range of students' perceptions and to help you become aware of ways of coping with these and of not alienating students unintentionally.

Poor prior experiences of learning

As a teacher, there is a tendency for you to focus on cognitive aspects of learning or skill development and the outcomes of learning. If you try to help students learn when they appear 'stuck', that is, when they are in the process of learning, you may be surprised at how anxious they become, how resistant they can be to your offer of help and how confused your explanations seem to leave them. If you have been a successful learner yourself you may underestimate how central emotions are to the process of learning.

When you later reflect on your session and question why students got 'stuck' and start to evaluate how the lesson went, you probably put this down to your poor teaching and try to think of different ways of presenting the topic next time. Although poor teaching is a possibility (as we shall discover later in the chapter), it is quite likely that the students' perceptions of that particular learning episode arose from poor experiences in the past. Of course, you cannot always anticipate what will trigger off what *you* perceive as an inappropriate emotional response to your requests, questions or explanations. Nevertheless, when you reflect, you need to explore different possibilities and not always look at things from a teacher's point of view but try to see them from the students' perspective by reflecting on what they say and on what they do.

When I asked a colleague to identify any skills or attributes they thought were beneficial for FE teachers in getting students to learn, the response was not quite what I was anticipating:

> I think you need to be somebody who actually likes adolescents, who can cope with 'toddler tantrums'! You need to have a sense of humour and be prepared to put in a lot of effort because the majority of our students are 16–19 and have very strong ideas about what they think is right in the world and when they begin college they usually see all adults as being a threat or not being people whom they can actually talk to. I think you need to overcome that.
>
> (Lecturer in Health and Social Care)

You can't necessarily predict that a simple question put to a student will result in 'toddler tantrums'. Sound advice is that the skill you require in this situation is to be someone a student can actually talk to and someone who can see things from the student's perspective.

However, one difficulty in trying to overcome the problems in getting students to learn is that the indicators which reveal whether or not students are uncomfortable with your teaching, or are just uneasy about being in the class for your particular subject and are not achieving, are so varied. Some students will tell you what the problem is straight away, for example:

- 'This reminds me of school. I hated school!'
- 'This is pointless. I've never got good marks in this. I'm rubbish at this.'

It is pretty evident that these students' perceptions of previous learning experiences are colouring their present one! But it's no use saying 'you're not at school now, grow up', as I heard an FE teacher telling a student recently.

A student's emotional response is likely to be triggered by a critical event in the past such as a being criticized by the teacher in front of the whole class when in primary school, or getting poor marks in an end of year examination when they were at secondary school, especially when they felt they'd worked hard and revised thoroughly. The emotions are brought to the surface years later almost without the students being aware of them. The feelings that a student has harboured against a particular teacher who humiliated them in front of their friends can suddenly rise to the surface – they experience the same sort of feelings that they had as a primary school pupil or re-live the sense of failure they experienced at secondary school. These emotions make a student fearful of the consequences of giving the wrong answer or being shown up in your class – even though the initial experience was years ago – and so they protect themselves by fending off situations that might prove embarrassing to them by getting in first with their 'excuses'. Understanding what the 'excuses' are probably hiding, enables you to be more patient in dealing with them and not responding emotionally yourself.

Other students may have had similar experiences when at school but their way of dealing with the emotional anxiety these experiences generate is different as they:

- Keep quiet and are reluctant to answer questions;
- Avoid joining in activities or discussing issues;
- Absent themselves from class without reason.

This behaviour means that the problems such students have with learning are not always obvious and their anxiety or fear of failure is not necessarily visible. However, their reluctance to communicate is still a way of making sure they don't show themselves up. A fear of being ridiculed as they have been in the past, or bullied by peers or teachers, is enough to make students keep their mouth shut and consequently appear sullen in group work. Perhaps daydreaming, rather than joining in, allows them to escape the pressures of the classroom and if the pressures become too much they may not even turn up to class. For mature students, the memory of failing the eleven plus examination which was used to select pupils for grammar school if they passed, but relegated them to a secondary modern school if they didn't, or having to leave school at 15 because they were not considered suitable to stay on by the school or were forced to leave because of their family circumstances, are past experiences that can colour their present attitudes to learning. These experiences mean that some mature students may be unsure of their ability to succeed and so try to melt into the background even when they are brave enough to venture into a classroom again.

There are also those students who do join in but their contributions are mainly negative or aggressive, such as:

- 'Why do you always pick on me? Ask someone else!'
- 'You haven't covered this. You can't expect me to answer these stupid questions.'
- 'If you think I'm doing another of your [blankety-blank] projects, you can have another [blankety-blank] think.'

The last remark was only one of a string of aggressive comments punctuated with expletives which prompted a lecturer in construction to recount the story in a training session – and it is shared with you in the case study below. He was so taken aback by the emotional outburst that he went over and talked to the student quietly and eventually found out the incident which triggered the aggressive response in the student happened over ten years ago.

A case of emotional outburst

One student told me during an activity, which was part of a BTEC National Certificate in Construction and which required some straightforward mathematical calculations to work out how many bricks to order to complete a particular building project, that as soon as anyone even mentioned calculations or counting he panicked. He explained that when he was in the infant school and supposed to be learning to count and weigh things he was messing around and playing with the counting bricks instead of working. His teacher got extremely cross, put him on a table on

---

his own and set him the task of counting how many grains there were in a 1lb of rice. He started off thinking it was a bit of a game, a bit of fun, but soon realized that it was going to take forever and he'd never be able to count up that far. He panicked and started crying and the teacher told him that he couldn't go home until he'd counted every last grain. He thought he'd be locked in the school all night on his own. He told me that when I said to the BTEC group that to cost the project they'd need to work out how many bricks they'd need to order for the structure he just flipped. He panicked about not being able to do the calculations. After he'd told me this, I just sat with him and went through the calculations step-by-step and he calmed down surprisingly quickly. (Lecturer in Construction Industries)

When you read the above case study you can imagine the little boy faced with a 1lb bag of rice – and your heart goes out to him. But stop and think for a minute about what the teacher had done and reflect if you've ever been guilty of using learning as a punishment and using threats to control students in class. You know you wouldn't treat an infant like that teacher did, but what about the young adults in your class who are messing around or playing up? It's so easy to 'lose it' when you're harassed or have been pushed to breaking point by disruptive or aggressive students, but the case study might help you realize the long-term consequences of such actions in class. So, before you dole out a punishment, threaten reprisals or get vindictive, remember you might be the subject of a learning horror story in ten years' time. Now that's not something that I expect you'd want to be remembered for!

Try this: Demonstrating empathy

Using 'A case of emotional outburst' above, identify the features of good practice that the FE teacher demonstrated in dealing with the student's emotional outburst. Check your own responses against the ones below.

The FE teacher's response demonstrates exemplary practice as he:

- dealt with the situation rather than ignored it;
- talked to the student calmly and quietly;
- made sure he was on his own when he talked to the student;
- listened to the student's side of things;
- helped the student with the troublesome calculations.

Most importantly, the teacher demonstrated to the student that having a problem with calculations is not a punishable offence. He showed the student that he was there to support their learning. Knowing that someone is there who understands their predicament and will help if necessary can often be the key thing that enables a student to realize that they can gradually overcome their resistance to learning.

No-one wants you to be a therapist in the classroom and that's certainly not your role, but empathizing with the student's predicament is important – rather then belittling it. Not only do FE teachers have to recognize when students are failing to learn, even when they don't have an emotional outburst, they also have to help students work through their educational hang-ups so that they can achieve in the future and not be stuck in the past.

Demonstrating empathy is not always easy to do, especially if students arrive with a hangover, or in a bad mood and obviously the worse for wear. It's not easy to empathize when a student can't grasp something during a session and you know you covered it the day they had 'bunked off'. It takes effort and patience to demonstrate empathy towards every student. When you are faced with students who arrive late, chat and waste time and don't hand in work on time, try to remember what Hanson (1996) found: when adults become students they tend to take on the characteristics of younger students and leave their responsible, mature selves outside the classroom door.

Poor experiences on a current programme

Despite the good example of teaching described in the last section, the quality of teaching is something about which students and teachers often hold differing perceptions. For example, they can often hold different values where various teaching methods are concerned. A sample of college students were asked to identify their worst current learning experiences. The responses came from students studying a range of subjects at various levels. Their worst current experiences included:

- A teacher just talking for two hours without a break or visual aids;
- Sitting in a lecture listening to the lecturer passively, and being bombarded with facts and figures;
- I don't enjoy lessons where we have to sit still and quiet for the whole lesson where the tutor is constantly speaking as I lose concentration;
- Purely sitting still for the entire length of lesson, not having opportunity for individual work.

The teachers involved in the evaluations above were obviously intent on getting their subject across, but all the students seem to recall is not the content of the lesson but their own inactivity. The teacher is doing all the work: researching the topic, preparing notes and summaries, organizing the information and doing any demonstrating or practical work. They probably spend hours preparing these sessions and their perspective is probably that they've planned thoroughly and have the facts at their fingertips for the students to take in. Unfortunately, from the students' perspective, these sessions are a 'turn off'. Their responses suggest that they do not appear to learn from simply having the facts of a subject presented to them by the teacher.

Try this: Developing rapport

Read the students' responses carefully and elicit from them what they want. Try to identify four things that would improve lessons:

1

2

3

4

The students provide the solutions themselves. How many things did you spot that the students identify?

- Not being quiet and listening for too long
- Not sitting still for the whole session
- Having a break in longer sessions
- Involvement in various activities so as not to lose concentration
- Using visual aids to help their learning
- Carrying out individual work
- Being active

Developing rapport is achieved by listening to what students say and talking to them about what helps them learn. Don't wait until you get adverse written evaluations from your students before you learn how you could improve your sessions. Build an understanding of what works for students by talking to them about their learning during sessions, and trying to see things from their point of view.

Expectations of the learning programme

You might get the impression from the last section that students do not want to know about your subject, but that is not true at all. Students expect to learn about a subject when they enrol on a course, but the way you go about getting them to enjoy it is critical, as the following evaluations show. Students were asked about times when teaching did not meet their expectations:

- Being taught by a lecturer sitting reading out a handout. [She] had no real subject knowledge and it showed;
- The lecturer is vague, long-winded and new to the format and learning outcomes of the course;
- When I have just been given information and not been talked through it;
- When we are given information and the task is not explained fully;
- When the tutors fail to share knowledge yet expect the student to know.

It is clear that students are keen to acquire subject knowledge and that they expect the FE teacher to be an expert in their subject and in the requirements of the course. The responses also show that students do not acquire subject knowledge just because they are told something. Learning needs to be active; it can be ineffective where passive exposure to other people's knowledge and skills is involved. As Rogers (2003: 12) puts it 'someone else cannot "learn" us'; students have to learn for themselves. There obviously needs to be some teacher input; students, as they identify above, need things explaining to them. The tricky part is getting the balance right between giving out information and getting the students to discover new knowledge or skills for themselves. You can't expect students to know about your subject unless you give them guidelines about what they are looking for, where to find it or how to do it. How much to tell students and how much you leave them to discover becomes easier to decide as you become more experienced at teaching a subject. Your observations, questioning and formative assessments of the students during the session are the key to getting this balance right.

Students evidently expect you to be an expert teacher and don't always make allowances for any inexperience. One student described how his expectations were not met because the teacher was a novice and obviously struggling to cope and feeling threatened by the experience. The student felt he had enrolled in a 'dysfunctional class'. His perception was that it was not the students who made it dysfunctional but the teacher. As FE teachers we tend to think that it is students who are dysfunctional and can empathize with a colleague who is struggling, but do we ever do anything practical and positive as colleagues or as a college to help 'dysfunctional teachers' or to improve the effectiveness of learning for students in groups that we don't teach? Do we ever consider that we are failing students when the quality of teaching doesn't meet their expectations? According to the research project 'The Transforming Learning Cultures in FE' (Teaching and Learning Research Project, 2005), improving the effectiveness of teaching entails modifying learning cultures: 'One way of doing this is to increase functional synergies and reduce dysfunctional tensions'. In other words, if we fail to coordinate some practical form of help for the struggling colleague to reduce the problem so that students' expectations are met, then perhaps we are unintentionally contributing to 'unequal opportunities' for the students in that particular group, as was suggested at the very beginning of this chapter.

Here are some other examples of how students' expectations about organizing, delivering and assessing subject content were not met by their teacher:

- A one-week course that was purely PowerPoint and had no structure;
- Learning about [subject] that I have no background, knowledge or interest in;
- Tutor [who] taught content not relevant to the assignment and was unclear about what was required for assessment;
- [Subject] was the most pointless assignment and I felt that it was irrelevant.

These four evaluations raise important questions about whether you should always react to evaluations and respond to students' requests or demands for a different approach to teaching or assessment. The quandary is whether you should follow your own judgement about how to organize your course and plan your sessions or take on board students' comments and change what you do. It's a professional dilemma, but you have to decide on the most appropriate course to follow. Before you decide, ask yourself the following questions:

- How did the methods you selected to present the session help students' learning?
- How did the sequence of the session help students to understand the content?
- How did the use of PowerPoint (or other resources) enhance the students' learning experience?
- How did the material covered in the session contribute both to development of subject knowledge and relevance to an assignment or assessment?

It's not easy, is it? But if you examine the questions you will notice that they focus on the *students'* learning experience. Your criteria for making a professional decision should be whether what you do enhances the students' learning. One problem though is that, despite teaching being a two-way process, it should leave the student in control of their learning (Petty, 2004) and what some FE teachers have a tendency to do is to try to take back some of that control. They need to reassure themselves that the curriculum is covered and the targets for achievement will be met. Very often they are concerned about covering everything that is in the lesson plan, even if they've run out of time. It's very easy to fall into this trap. I can remember feeling that I needed to 'cover' everything in class and as a lesson drew near its end I would often hear myself saying 'just before you go it's important to know . . .'. Of course, the students had had enough by then and had switched off, so the mini-lecture that I considered so vital fell on deaf ears. How much better it would have been to have suggested that the students research by reading or looking up the information on the internet themselves between sessions and sharing their findings in discussion in the next session.

The pressure to stick to your lesson plan and include everything in the order you've set out is enormous – and flexibility in delivery is something that the demands of Ofsted inspections seem to be driving out. FE teachers are concerned not to seem to be deviating from their objectives. What you have to remember is that students' expectations have to be met as well.

Nevertheless, teachers regularly take control by organizing the programme, selecting the topic, choosing the methods, designing the assignments and identifying the criteria for assessment. I am not suggesting that FE teachers should relinquish all responsibility and not have any input into sessions and that lessons should begin each time with a discussion about what the students want to do, as Rogers (1983) seems to advocate. With 20 or so students and probably as many different views, this would mean that you would probably end up with a session that became a 'free-for-all'. Most likely no one would end up satisfied and arguments would ensue about whom you listened to and whose requests you responded to! I wouldn't advocate leaving students completely responsible for their learning, but would see it as more of a shared responsibility.

You would think that student presentations would be a good method of choice for FE teachers as they relinquish control to students. They are often included in courses nowadays and FE teachers perceive them as an excellent vehicle for developing key skills. However, students have a different perception of presentations when you ask them to evaluate these:

- 'I have found that presentations are not useful and create a lot of extra work.'
- 'Doing presentations. I don't like them.'

When you are aware of adverse student perceptions to their giving presentations, do you just stop including these in your sessions or do you try to explain the value of them to your students? It's bit like getting school children to eat healthy school dinners. There is a consensus that a healthy diet is important but children always find ways to get out of eating school dinners. Does that mean that there has to be a return to feeding them rubbish? I don't think so! But this analogy does bring home the fact that students' perceptions and teachers' perceptions of learning and teaching differ. To ease the students into presentations, it might be preferable to focus on allowing them the freedom to choose their topics rather than labour the point about the importance of key skills, as that is a bit like trying to persuade a child that green vegetables are good for them. With freedom of choice comes responsibility. So, for example, the students might be given responsibility for their own success in a qualification through some control over what they include in their presentation, yet without control over the method of assessment.

Such decisions about what will be learnt and how it will be learnt obviously require professional judgement and one way in which you can shift control between yourself and your students is through your selection of teaching methods. The range of students' perceptions presented in this chapter indicate that it is *teacher control* – through the choice of formal teaching methods – that they have a problem with in lessons, and an important factor in 'getting the buggers to learn' is to allow more *student control*. Minton (2005: 150) provides an excellent continuum depicting a range of teaching methods from 'Teacher control' to 'Least control' on which to base your decisions.

Try this: Encouraging student control

Check your old lesson plans and then use Minton's model to identify whether you are a 'control freak' or 'student-friendly' and encouraging of student control.

Teacher control		Lecture
	Less control	Demonstration
		Discussion – structured
		Discussion – unstructured
		Seminar
		Tutorial
	Shared control	Practical
		Simulation and games
		Role play
		Resource-based learning
		Films/TV programmes
		Visits
	Student control	Distance learning/Flexistudy
		Discovery projects/research
Least control		Real-life experience

(Minton, 2005: 150, Fig 16.1 Teacher control – student control)

When questioned about what they consider to be rewarding learning experiences, students' evaluations showed that the teaching methods they prefer give them control over their learning:

- It was rewarding learning about creativity at college and then using my new knowledge to give my own children new experiences at home.
- I think learning is most rewarding when you can easily relate what you are learning about to what you do at work every day and you are encouraged to use workplace examples in your essays and practicals.
- Hands-on learning, I find, is the best way I learn: visits, activities, work placement.
- Going on trips, for example, visiting an industrial site, a workplace or a conference.
- Being awarded a distinction for an assignment after researching everything and working on my own.

These responses identify methods which Minton classifies towards the end of the continuum where there is 'least control' by the teacher, for example, visits, projects/research and real-life experience. It is interesting to note that the model shows that as a teacher you have least control over 'real-life experiences'. This will be discussed in the next section.

Expectations of themselves

When students enrol on a course or sign up for some training and appear in your classroom or workshop for the first time, they bring with them their own set of attitudes about your subject, perspectives about teaching and expectations of themselves as learners. A student's personality, disposition towards learning and their experiences all contribute to the value they place on learning and how they will respond to your teaching. It is 'real-life experience' that has made these students what they are – and that is something you have least control over.

It is very difficult to know exactly what it feels like to be one of the students in your class and know how they perceive your class and what their expectations are. Students are complex and subject to many influences:

> ... each is the result of how far environment and experience have promoted or inhibited growth, realized or stunted potential, and shaped his or her self-image.
>
> (Minton, 2005: 5)

Students only attend college for a small part of their life and family attitudes towards education and employment, along with peer pressures and previous teaching, are very powerful forces in determining their expectations about college. Social constraints, such as whether education is valued by their community, themselves and other family members, or job prospects in the local area and whether there are job opportunities in their chosen career, are influences that shape the individual and which in turn make them have greater or lesser expectations of themselves and of their college course. The way a student behaves around college and what they perceive as acceptable in class is shaped by their background and, in particular, their peer group. If students are employed then the demands and expectations of their employers about qualifications will also affect their expectations of what they can achieve at college.

Students, therefore, bring with them an attitude towards themselves, and Dweck (1999) promotes the importance of teachers being aware of the influence of an individual student's self concept in relation to learning. Some students may regard themselves as having little ability and only do as much as is needed to get by. Some put their success in learning down to luck and feel their achievements are down to things outside of their control, for example, easy questions in an examination. A student's own interests influence the way they approach your subject and the fact that they chose it in the first place. If they are interested, or need the qualification, then their expectations of success will be high, but may not always be realistic.

However you deal with this, it is fraught with difficulties, for example:

- 'Being told I may not pass GCSE [subject] – this lack of belief from a teacher resulted in me feeling incapable of achieving a grade.'
- 'I was keen to pass [module] but the poor marks the teacher gave me made my confidence in what I could do low.'

As a teacher, you try to be truthful and not build up false hopes in the student, but despite your good intentions it seems that students can perceive feedback from you as de-motivating. There are mixed views from researchers about whether it is the effort students put in, their innate ability or the difficulty of a particular task they have to carry out that determines whether they achieve. One view, which many FE teachers would subscribe to, is that effort pays off and they encourage their students to put this in with feedback such as:

- 'Work a bit harder';
- 'Keep up the good work';
- 'With a bit more effort you'd get a higher grade';
- 'It's worth the effort in the long run'.

However, Ecclestone (2002) reveals another view when discussing students' motivation, which is that others dispute that effort pays off and raises the standard of a student's work, and they also think that too much emphasis is placed on encouraging students to put in more effort as there is no evidence that effort necessarily improves work rates or performance. So, if you believe this, it's no good encouraging students to work harder. So, what can you do?

One way is to be aware of how individual students construct their reality. Let me explain. There is an approach to learning that suggests that the individual has to constantly renegotiate who they are if they are to grow and develop. According to what is called a 'constructive-developmental' perspective of adult growth (Drago-Severson, 2004) students actively make sense of their experiences (that's the constructive part of the term) and the ways that they do it develop gradually and progressively over time (that's the developmental part of the term). So, the way that you can help students learn is to identify where they are in this developmental process. Although this perspective implies that personal growth happens in chronological order, it is important to realize that students of similar ages or at similar stages in life aren't necessarily at the same development point. Although Drago-Severson tells us that there are six different levels of making sense of experiences – or ways of constructing reality – three are particularly relevant to FE students. These ways of knowing are defined as:

- Instrumental
- Socializing
- Self-authoring.

Although these definitions might mean something to their creators, as they stand they don't appear that helpful in getting students to learn. To help them mean something to you, have a go at the following activity.

Try this: Recognizing developmental diversity

To become aware of the developmental diversity of students within your group, identify whether they respond by instrumental, socializing or self-authoring learning. To find this out, what you should do is three quite simple things:

1. Ask students to describe themselves.
2. Listen to their questions which should reveal their concerns about learning.
3. Listen to their questions which should reveal their concerns about their progress.

Use the questions in the following table as a guide.

LEARNERS	DESCRIPTION OF SELF (1)	CONCERNS ABOUT LEARNING (2)	QUESTIONS ABOUT PROGRESS (3)
INSTRUMENTAL	Describes appearance, likes and dislikes, job, car, etc., in concrete terms, e.g. I'm very tall and like swimming.	Will I get penalized if I don't do something, e.g. hand in work on time?	What's in it for me? College course taken to acquire something: a better job/more money.
SOCIALIZING	Describes abstract qualities such as sensitivity, shyness, e.g. I often feel confused.	Will you still like me if I don't do well in your subject/get good results?	What do you think I should know? College course is taken to be someone: a good student or employee.
SELF-AUTHORING	Describes how different they are from others and provides an evaluation of self, e.g. I'm the sort of person who likes to do things to the best of my ability.	Am I achieving my goals and reaching for my ideals?	What is important for me to know to keep learning and growing? College course taken to become someone: a competent and more enriched person.

(Adapted from Drago-Severson, 2004: Table 210, pp. 29–30)

The point of the above activity is not to categorize or label students, but rather to become aware that their levels of development are all very different, even in the same group. If you listen to the students carefully, for example, when they're asking for help, complaining about lessons, having a moan about college work, etc., then it's not too difficult to relate their questions and comments to the 'constructive-developmental'

91

model of adult growth. When you do this, you learn more about the stage a student is at and can begin to understand things from their perspective. You can reassure them about their concerns and their progress in a way that is meaningful to them. But more importantly, you can help them to move to the next developmental stage. The pace of this will vary from student to student and is likely to be gradual over a whole year or even longer, so don't expect instant results.

If you want students to move from thinking about things in concrete terms, that is, in terms of black or white, good or bad, then your feedback needs to introduce the idea that there can be two points of view at the same time; it's not a question of one thing or another. An example of this would be when a student talks about a piece of work and says something like 'I know it's a fail, it can't possibly be a pass'. Your response would be to identify parts of the work that are at a pass level and tell them why, and then identify parts that would make it a fail and tell them why and how they could improve. If the subject area is more practical and the student complains 'It's all a mess, none of it works, it all looks wrong!', again you can explain that some parts work fine, other bits are OK and there is just one particular bit that needs working on. You establish that one piece or work or one project can be both good and bad at the same time. Your feedback helps students shift their thinking from concrete to abstract, that is, from thinking they'll be penalized for their work, to realizing that the teacher can identify both things that work and areas for improvement – that it's not all bad.

Focus on students

It is very easy to give advice and guidance and make 'getting the buggers to learn' sound simple, but time is needed to develop such skills. The questions you should put to your students might be simple ones but you will need to gain experience in knowing when to pose them and when to challenge or support students. Getting it wrong just adds to your problems. That said, one of the most beneficial things that you can do to encourage students is to create opportunities for them to identify positive qualities, skills and abilities in themselves. Many people find it hard to take a compliment and it's the same with students, so you need to encourage them to talk about the positive aspects of their work. You can ask them what skills are required to achieve such work and encourage them to realize that these are the skills that they possess. It doesn't matter if you have to struggle to find something positive to talk to the student about at first because once they have recognized that they have some skill their self-esteem will grow and they will be on an upward, rather than a downward, spiral and more inclined to engage in further learning tasks.

Getting the buggers to learn: Focusing on students

- Students have their own ideas about what teachers and teaching should be like.
- Students have high expectations of their teachers.
- Students' perceptions of past learning experiences may colour their present attitude to learning.
- Try to cope with students' emotional outbursts calmly.
- You can't 'learn' students – they have to be active in their own learning.
- When choosing teaching methods, select those which encourage 'student control'.
- The student's context and environment shape their self-image.
- There is wide developmental diversity in any student group.
- Talk to and listen to students and allow the 'student voice' to be heard.

In Chapter 6 the importance of the teaching role and ways in which FE teachers can contribute to students' learning are addressed.

6

WHY ARE TEACHERS SO IMPORTANT FOR STUDENTS' LEARNING?

In this chapter you will find that teachers are important for students' learning because:

- Teachers provide the sought-after yet elusive 'value-added' factor through facilitating students' progress;
- Teachers help students navigate their own learning journey;
- Teachers can focus on both short-term and long-term objectives which contribute to student development;
- Teachers can discriminate between learning as task-conscious or learning-conscious;
- You can't leave every aspect of students' learning to 'real-life' experience. Teachers devise tasks and assessments to extend students' knowledge and skills.

You will also find ideas about how to think about lesson planning, reflect on your skills in formative assessment, and the importance of integrating both teaching, learning and assessment and the cognitive, affective and social dimensions of teaching and learning.

Teaching quality

Quality teaching is about creatively managing the personal experiences and worlds of the individual learners, as well as staying in touch with the nuances of the group dynamic. It requires pedagogic decision-making to be made swiftly on the wing and draws on the historic stock of previous exchanges the group has held in its collective memory.

(Cockburn, 2005: 379)

Cockburn's notion of quality teaching is one where the decisions made by the insightful teacher are underpinned by events that have bonded the group together and draw on the goodwill these have generated within the group. He asserts that the greater the artistry of the teacher, the more intangible the decisions and actions become and, therefore, the less apparent they are to an outside observer. This is a real problem when building a case for the importance of the teacher in 'getting the buggers to learn' because the talents and skills, which Cockburn contends form the keystone of quality teaching, are not automatically evident. The creative and inventive nature of quality teaching is implicit and although it is generally understood and appreciated by the student group, unfortunately it is very often not recognized by observers, managers and colleagues.

Similarly, there is evidence that FE teachers routinely engage in working well beyond their job descriptions in their attempts to get high achievement rates. The researchers term this practice 'underground working' which they describe as a risky process that entails

> putting the students' interests before the dictates of bureaucracy, and often before the personal needs of the tutors concerned . . . and giving more of themselves as people than the job strictly demanded.
>
> (Gleeson, 2005: 241)

The 'underground working' suggests that the extra time and effort put in by FE teachers – and which enables the students to achieve their best and also makes it possible for the college to achieve its targets – is somehow secretive and hidden and, once again, the work that FE teachers do to get students to learn is experienced by students but goes unrecognized by officialdom.

Over the years there have been various policies and initiatives which are intended to encourage independent learning and to minimize the importance of the presence of the FE teacher in the classroom, for example, resource-based learning, self-directed study and computer-aided learning. Such initiatives were designed so that students could work independently in workshops or through distance learning, for example, in the workplace or at home. The FE teachers' skills were still required to develop the materials and work-packs and to carry out assessment, but the students' learning was overseen by a technician, learning-support assistant or a workplace supervisor rather than a teacher. My experience in managing college-based and outreach workshops is that not only was the success of such ventures heavily reliant on the quality of the resources developed by the subject teachers, but also that an individual student's progress was dependent on the quality of the personal skills and attributes of the support staff. It became clear that to deal with student queries effectively, specialist learner support was becoming increasingly important – rather than less important – as FE colleges moved towards student-centred education through modularization and workshop delivery. My conclusion was that facilitating students' learning was a role for the qualified FE subject teacher (Steward, 2003).

Tickle's research also places emphasis on the identity of the person who facilitates learning and he says:

> It is also the 'who' that denies the possibility of standardization and ensures the rich texture of educational encounters.
>
> (Tickle, 2000: 83)

College managers, however, appear to ignore the importance of *who* ensures a rich experience for the student in what Tickle calls 'educational encounters' (for example, in workshops, tutorials or classrooms) and seem to make the assumption that the FE teacher's presence is unnecessary in student-centred education. I acknowledge that quality teaching is not always easy to observe as the teacher's actions can be intangible. Nevertheless, the importance of *who* teaches them is certainly recognized by students. To support this claim, my experience and research suggests that it is the role the FE teachers play and their personal skills and attributes that contribute to students' learning and make a difference (Steward, 2003).

It is the FE teachers who provide the 'value-added' dimension which college managers appreciate through evidence of students' growth, progress and improvement between course entry and course exit, whatever their level or ability. But if college managers cannot perceive a significant difference in quality between a technician and an FE teacher as a facilitator of learning, then the FE teacher's job is surely in a precarious position. It is our job as professionals to make sure that teachers provide 'value-added' for the benefit of students and for the college.

There is no doubt that the invisibility of much of their expertise contributes to FE teachers today being fearful of the way teaching and learning is being transformed by technology and fearful of the impact of this on their jobs. Tickle's argument that it is *who* facilitates learning that is important is confirmed by Leach (2006) who also contends that without teachers any innovation is going to falter. For example, if it is to be successful, the personalization of learning which is currently being promoted means taking the personal needs of students into account. This is where teachers' knowledge and skills are invaluable, as the starting point for delivering personalized learning is to tailor the curriculum to meet students' needs and it is FE teachers who have the expertise to know how best to address those needs. Their expertise comes from their knowledge of the different ways students approach learning, from their knowledge of the principles of effective teaching and learning, and from their experience of ways of applying the principles in a new context – thus making the curriculum more accessible and responsive. However desirable this approach sounds, cynics may say that the personalization agenda is down to economics, and Gregory observes:

> Flexibility and accessibility do not, contrary to popular view, enhance the learning experience. Primarily they facilitate the economics of education ...
>
> (Gregory, 2002: 183)

Financial necessity is no doubt one of the drivers of the personalization agenda, but notwithstanding economic benefits for colleges, it is my experience, gained through managing self-study workshops, that they were transformed from virtual production lines in which students 'rolled-on' and 'rolled-off' to a more effective, flexible and accessible 'learning encounter' for students through the personal attributes and skills demonstrated by FE teachers and the individual differences between teachers. Introducing savings which impede the value-added dimension of students' learning and disadvantage students must be false economy.

Technology has the power to change the nature of teaching, to switch it from whole-class teaching to more one-to-one sessions which are more flexible and engaging. To keep up-to-date, FE teachers have to manage the switch between group dynamics and individual learning and make considerable pedagogic decisions. According to Morrison, there is an:

> ... evolving consensus that e-learning requires more, rather than less attention to pedagogy, curriculum management and the role of tutors and that this should apply as much to 'bite-sized chunks' of individualised learning as it does for other forms ... the relation between teaching and learning, as traditionally conceived, is being transformed.
>
> (Morrison, 2005: 409)

The transformation of teaching that Morrison refers to demands different personal skills and attributes to those required for traditional classroom teaching and this change means that you must keep up-to-date. Further, there are costs in terms of the FE teacher's sense of self, ability to adjust and feelings of insecurity. FE teachers have to change and develop as approaches to teaching and learning change and develop. Instead of considering themselves as taken-for-granted by college managers and policymakers, an important role for FE teachers today is to strengthen the link between teaching, learning and assessment and focus on how they can contribute to the 'value-added' dimension of students learning, whether it be through traditional teaching or e-learning.

Helping students to navigate their own learning journey

The metaphor of a journey to represent learning is well-established in education. There is a commonsense understanding of learning as motion, for example, as movement, growth, action and activity. The questions that the use of this figure of speech raise for the FE teacher are:

- Just where is the journey taking the student to?
- How will you know if the student is on the right track?
- How will you know if and when the student has arrived at the destination?

Students tend to focus on their immediate goals or objectives – not their destination – but the FE teacher has to focus not only on immediate, short-term objectives but also on long-term objectives.

The short-term objectives students tend to focus on relate to the activities and tasks students are engaged in during every lesson. These are important to provide evidence that the curriculum is being addressed, but they are even more important to ensure that students' knowledge and skills are being extended and developed. It is not enough to look around your classroom or workshop and feel content because students are all busy working. It's all too easy to give students lots to do to keep a sense of order in the classroom and to feel pleased when they are getting on and keeping relatively quiet. If you have a trouble-some group then this is an important first step – which you should congratulate yourself on achieving. But 'getting the buggers to learn' requires more than just keeping students occupied and quiet. Just because students are completing tasks and getting them right does not necessarily mean that they are extending their knowledge or skills. You should check that they understand what they are doing and check that they are progressing and absorbing new knowledge or skills and the way to do this is through formative assessment during the session – you haven't got time to sit and mark, or complete record sheets!

Formative assessment works best when it is informal. It is not about marking work or giving marks out of ten for tasks, but observing what students are doing, then giving specific feedback. I know students tend to like quizzes as informal assessment, but these just check what has already been learnt, whereas formative assessment provides feedback about a student's performance and gives them the opportunity to think about what they are doing and perhaps change or adapt their ideas. The teacher's job is to diagnose what's going on and to confirm everything's fine or provide a remedy if necessary. Chatting to pupils about how they're progressing, rather than shouting out orders across the room to get students back on task, enables you to connect with the way they are approaching the task and how they are coping with it. If you watch what students are doing, talk to them and listen carefully to their responses, you can encourage them to talk about how they're learning and express their understanding. You must give students time to respond to your feedback, so don't leave checking work to the end of the session but instead give specific information and guidance about how to proceed or improve throughout the session.

Formative assessment is particularly helpful in getting reluctant learners, for example those with a tendency to put off starting a task or to stop and chat or give up easily, to stay on task. It either reinforces that they are on the right lines which reassures students, or feeds in ways to sort out problems if they aren't. Either way, it helps them get on.

Meeting your short-term objectives and addressing the students' immediate objectives requires considerable skill and tact on your part. You have to 'think on your feet' and draw on your expertise as a subject specialist as well as demonstrate your teaching skills, because if you give inappropriate feedback or intervene at the wrong moment, you will confuse the student rather than help them and they'll get frustrated.

Try this: Supporting and challenging

Reflect on a recent lesson you taught and analyse how you extended students' knowledge and skills. Think of examples when you:

- Provided feedback which gave specific guidance on how to improve and what you did to support and help students to work on your suggestions;
- Provided feedback which challenged the students and how they responded and rose to the challenge.

Your professional competence is needed to support short-term objectives, but whilst you are dealing with these you also need to keep in mind long-term objectives. Even though the students are only focused on the task in hand, you cannot lose sight of where the students' learning journey is taking them and what they'll need to reach their destination. An important part of your role as an FE teacher is to remember that in your daily work you 'are shaping long-term life-chances and identities, as well as working towards immediate targets for performance' (Pollard, 2002: 83). In the hustle and bustle of the classroom or workshop you have to foster each student's confidence in themselves as a learner and also be aware of your responsibility to enable students to develop as people who are adaptable, self-assured and have gained the vocational skills they need for future employment.

It's not easy to keep long-term objectives in mind, such as preparing students for the workplace or for their future roles in life, when you're busy dealing with the day-to-day demands of students in the classroom. If students are persistently failing in their short-term objectives and in the tasks you set in class their sense of themselves is damaged and leads to low self-esteem. But, if you provide opportunities for successful learning through your formative feedback (which provides students with the chance to correct their work themselves and continue on the right lines rather than give up) then students feel a sense of achievement and their confidence develops, and they can begin to focus on long-term objectives for themselves. Positive classroom experiences accumulate over the sessions and contribute to a student's enjoyment of learning.

Hager (2005) suggests that the way we describe learning makes a difference to how we think about teaching. If you think about your role as helping students to navigate their own learning journey, as suggested in this chapter, then the assumption is that learning involves travelling along a path and that you have to do this with some destination in mind, perhaps a product achieved at the end of the journey. This may give students the idea that when they've got to the end of the course, or achieved their qualification, then this is the end of learning. The metaphor that Hager prefers is not one that implies learning as 'acquisition', or even 'participation', but that implies 'construction'. He proposes that learning should be thought of as 'preparation for future learning' and this term captures the idea that you encourage students to engage in classroom activities not only to complete the curriculum requirements or meet the performance criteria, but also to develop as learners. This holistic way of thinking about learning suggests that as an FE teacher you have to help students not only build their vocational skills and knowledge but also to build their learning skills and accept that further learning is always going to be required throughout life.

Task-conscious and learning-conscious learning

As if thinking about both short-term and long-term objectives wasn't enough to keep you occupied in sessions, you also have to think about the nature of the tasks you use to achieve these objectives. Rogers (2003) proposed that there are two distinct forms of learning:

- **Task-conscious learning.** The student is not conscious of the fact that they are learning, but conscious of the task they are doing. The significance of this for the teacher is that the student does not recognize what they are doing is learning and they focus on completing the task for its own sake, not as learning for some future activity. Task-conscious learning is important in everyday life as it enables students to cope with new situations they face. Practical tasks that you design for students will not necessarily be seen by all of them as learning unless you intervene. Often students just concentrate on completing the task for its own sake and are glad when it's done and probably don't relate it to any other part of their programme or course. All they are concerned with is the immediate task completion and to get it over with. Your attention is drawn to this task-conscious approach to learning when students rush through their work without much thinking and call out such things as:

- 'I've finished. What shall I do now?'
- 'Is that it? Can I pack up now?'
- 'That didn't take long. Can we have our break now?'
- **Learning-conscious learning.** This approach to learning is more formal and the student is conscious that the task they are doing is actually intended as learning. The teacher's goal is to help make students *more* aware of this and to draw the students' attention to lesson objectives, learning outcomes or performance criteria at appropriate points as they are doing the task. Teachers can encourage this approach to learning by breaking the curriculum into topics or themes and then evaluating how much has been learned by checking the activities and projects against the goals set. A teacher's formative assessment of the task should encourage the student to understand that learning itself is the task and raise their awareness of the strategies and techniques they are using to learn by getting the students to talk about these and identify them. Through conversations like this, students gradually become more aware of the process of learning and how they learn. Remember too, even though students learn from the teacher, they also learn from their peers and others who are involved with the students, so collaboration and sharing contributes to an individual's learning rather than detracts from it. Before you tell students to 'stop talking and get on', listen to what they are talking about. You might be surprised to find that their talk is sometimes related to the task they are involved and not last night's activities.

Rogers doesn't advocate one approach to learning rather than the other, but – just like short-term and long-term objectives – he advocates that both approaches to learning have their own value. However, in your teaching you can demonstrate to students the relationship between actively doing something and learning from it. This is most successful when the students' specific learning needs and the experiences they bring with them are recognized. The way this is done, according to Rogers (2003), must depend on the teacher, the subject, the context and the particular group of learners. You also need to understand the different ways in which students are learning outside the classroom (this was addressed in Chapter 1) and incorporate elements of that learning into your lessons plans and learning programme.

The next step is to try to see if you can integrate all these factors into your session planning. A model I have found extremely useful was devised for schools, but I have adapted this for FE students. See if it works for you!

Try this: Thoughtful planning

Use the model below, which has been adapted from Pollard (2002: 213), to help you plan a session involving new learning. Think about the five phases in the model as you structure your session. The possible processes should give you some ideas about the tasks required to achieve the purposes.

	PURPOSES	POSSIBLE PROCESSES
1. ORIENTATION (Direction and point of reference for starting)	Arousing students' interest and curiosity. • Ensures that the students are focused on the topic and are motivated	• Introducing • Explaining • Discussing • Relating to experience
2. ELICITATION/ STRUCTURING (Drawing out ideas and using students' input to plan)	Helping students to find out and clarify what they think. • Enables the teacher to assess students' understanding in order to plan appropriate next steps	• Questioning • Discussing • Predicting
3. INTERVENTION/ RESTRUCTURING (Getting students involved in tasks and challenge or support)	Encouraging students to test, develop, extend or replace their ideas or skills. • Provides opportunities to engage actively in learning tasks	• Practising • Observing • Measuring • Recording • Speculating

	PURPOSES	POSSIBLE PROCESSES
	• Enables the teacher to observe students and, by assessing their skill and understanding, to make appropriate teaching interventions	
4. REVIEW (Reassess and talk to students about learning)	Helping students to evaluate the significance and value of what they have done. • Offers a chance for students to take stock of their learning and for the teacher to guide them in consolidating their understanding • Provides an opportunity for the teacher to assess new learning and to consider the next steps	• Recording • Discussing • Explaining • Hypothesizing • Reporting • Evaluating
5. APPLICATION (Highlight relevance for future assignment, workplace, etc.)	Helping students to relate what they have learned to their everyday lives. • Enables the students to locate new learning meaningfully in the wider context of their work and home lives • Provides an opportunity for the teacher to reinforce and consolidate points	• Relating to experience • Discussing • Interpreting

(Adapted from Pollard, 2002: 313, Fig 14.2 Phases of teaching, learning and assessment)

Five phases of teaching and learning are distinguished in the above model. The significance of this model for FE teachers is that the five phases build on students' existing knowledge and skills and relate their learning to their own experiences. The model starts by drawing on students' previous experiences and finishes with students applying new experiences, knowledge and skills to their everyday life. Each phase includes formative assessment by the teacher to promote learning. Interweaving continuous assessment with teaching and learning enables the teacher to understand how students are thinking and to extend the students' knowledge and skills by challenging and supporting them as appropriate.

Extending students' knowledge and skills

The tutor [is] a major influence on the quality of learning and the student experience.

(Gleeson, 2005: 241)

FE teachers draw on a variety of vocational skills and experiences, and professional knowledge of teaching and learning, incorporating these into learning programmes to promote their students' learning. However, the diversity of the sector means that the 'one model fits all' approach to lesson preparation and delivery in the Learning and Skills Sector, which is often prescribed by trainers and policymakers, is inadequate. A more individual approach to teaching would not only draw on the FE teacher's vocational and workplace experience, their personal skills and individual creativity but would also take into account the different requirements of diverse vocational provision and employer expectations to be found in any FE college. The following examples show just how diverse the sector is and that, for example, where a competitive climate would be abhorrent in teaching students with learning difficulties and disabilities, it might be acceptable when preparing students to be successful in the commercial world of hairdressing and beauty therapy. The difference between teaching areas and between students is something to be celebrated and it is what makes the FE sector unique.

Try this: Celebrating difference

Notice how diverse the following teaching and assessment are, and see if you can pick up any ideas to adapt and use in your own teaching area.

VOCATIONAL AREA	FE TEACHERS' SUCCESSFUL STRATEGIES
Public Services	'Pass in Class': students prepare interactive, hands-on activities using task sheets, PowerPoint with video footage and music, photographs from visits, maps, etc. which they present to the group, and can choose to have such activities assessed. This develops different skills to those assessed in outdoor expeditions and is a way of developing interpersonal relations in the group.
Retail	Using 'Blackboard' and IT facilities, build up a range of resources which relate to the subject and that the students are interested in, and provide 'short and snappy' activities. Use different ones for different students and treat each student individually.
Hospitality and Catering ABC Level 1	Get students to choose everyday meals to cook from ingredients they may have at home and support them by taking on preparation responsibility so that they all enjoy the practical aspects of the lessons and can complete the activities themselves. Share the results.
Art – Young Offenders	Success depends on informality and making the students relaxed, so plenty of laughter. Using IT provides opportunities for positive activities. E.g. I noticed how one student, whom I'd never met before, didn't want to participate. He had a skateboard, hoodie, etc. so I got him to do a project on graffiti which he enjoyed and engaged with.
Hairdressing	Hold a competition on 'hair ups' which is something the students have to be assessed on. This activity makes learning enjoyable. It gives the students a chance to work on something together and doesn't appear patronizing to them, as some college

	projects seem to. They rise to the challenge and really enjoy the competition.
Animal Science	Encourage students to organize their own demonstration for 'animal handling', make a video of it and use this on Open Day. They will take ownership of the display, which is related to learning outcomes so they can use it for assessment.

After reading the examples, you can see why the 'one model fits all approach' doesn't work in FE colleges. Students respond to teaching that is both creative and relevant to their vocational area and which they can enjoy. Notice how the examples show how successful FE teachers can integrate teaching, learning and assessment into activities and combine thinking skills, emotional and social dimensions of learning.

Focusing on teaching

It is clear from reading this chapter that learning involves a 'complicated interaction between a number of elements' and Rogers (2003) discusses how learning comprises three integrated dimensions: the cognitive, the affective and the social. Successful teachers aim to address all three dimensions and integrate teaching, learning and assessment – but the way each of them does this will result in different strategies and activities. Each of them brings their own experiences, skills and attributes to teaching.

Getting the buggers to learn: Focusing on teaching

- Quality teaching is recognized and appreciated by students.
- A teacher's extra time and effort is rewarded by students' achievements.
- There is no one single approach to teaching that will provide answers for the teacher.

- Integrating teaching, learning and assessment throughout sessions helps students to stay on task.
- Teachers need to be aware of the interaction between cognitive, affective and social dimensions of learning.
- Student-centred learning flourishes with support from a subject teacher.
- An important role of the teacher is to prepare the student for future learning.
- The value-added dimension of students' learning is achieved through teachers facilitating students' progress.
- E-learning requires teaching expertise and curriculum management just as much as traditional classroom teaching.

Chapter 7 looks at change in the Learning and Skills Sector and discusses ways FE teachers can manage change.

7

WHY ARE THINGS ALWAYS CHANGING?

In this chapter you will find that the Learning and Skills Sector is a key agent of change in today's society:

- Policy reviews advocate new approaches to vocational education;
- Academics and experts introduce new ways of thinking about teaching and learning;
- Employers develop new technologies, products and markets and require employees to have different skills and knowledge;
- Colleges have to be adaptable to survive.

In this chapter you will also find ideas about the importance of keeping up-to-date and ways to engage in professional learning.

Change is always with us

You must keep up to date. Education, institutions and methods of teaching and learning have been forced to change in order to keep pace with the world they serve. Many of those changes have perhaps been arbitrary, the result of ideological processes rather than pressures from employment in a technological society. Yet there is no sign that changes will become less painful in future.

(Minton, 2005: 334)

If FE colleges are considered a driving force of change by government, policymakers, academics and employers, then they have the potential to be innovative and inspirational centres of tertiary education for thousands of students in the UK. But, as Minton points out, change is painful and educational change is a complicated business. The paradox is that in a rapidly changing society, FE teachers are often reluctant to change their practices. Teaching in innovative ways often requires more energy and extra time, which those who are just coping with challenging learners may be short of. Even newcomers to the Learning and Skills Sector may find that pressure to cover the curriculum, and the requirements of external examinations and qualification frameworks, leave them little flexibility to try out new methods of teaching. Sometimes the reluctance of FE teachers to change is reinforced by existing organizational structures and colleges, which are not always ideal learning environments for teachers.

But, however painful change may be, you can't lock yourself in your classroom or workshop and take no notice of what is going on in the world outside. Education policies, the changing nature of employment and employment opportunities, shifting social values and new technology are all influences on the local culture, your college, your teaching and your students. These critical forces influence every part of the FE sector. For example, a policy that promotes educational inclusion may mean that students who may not have traditionally engaged in education over the age of 16 are now enrolled at college and, as a consequence, individual differences amongst students in your classroom or workshop may be wider and teaching methods that were once successful may no longer suffice. Obliging 16-year-olds to remain in education or work-based training until they are 18 years old or face a system of penalties is a contentious policy. You would not for one minute question the right of students to continue their education, but you might question how you can be successful in 'getting the buggers to learn' if a new cohort of students is being forced to stay in education and is in college under compulsion. You would probably agree that those who are the most challenging students have the most to gain from continuing with their education – but they are unlikely to be compliant and the most likely to be disruptive or drop out if they are not enjoying the experience. Your usual teaching methods will be under severe strain. Whether you like it or not, as an FE teacher you are subject to critical forces of change within your classroom or workshop that emanate from the wider environment and are beyond your individual control.

But all is not lost! Your classroom or workshop is a key learning setting; not only for your students but also for you (Hoban, 2002). You become aware of problems that change brings and to resolve them you have to look beyond the walls of your classroom or workshop and open the door to the world outside for possible solutions. Surprisingly, identifying a problem is a really good start for professional learning. If you are unsure about getting students to learn, you need to hear about new policies, read about new research or observe the way others in the FE sector do things so that you can draw on these different ideas and incorporate them into your professional practice to improve your teaching and students' learning.

Changing policies

Recommendations contained within government or sector policy documents can have a significant impact on the way colleges operate. In recent years, the government asked Sir Andrew Foster to carry out an independent review of the future role of FE colleges (Foster, 2005). Foster's key recommendation was that the focus of colleges should be on the provision of skills and ensuring employability for students. Although the report stated that courses that contribute to social inclusion, academic courses or professional development courses would not be automatically excluded, there is already evidence of a change in provision in these areas. Foster also proposed a more streamlined Learning and Skills Council with its national and regional roles being clarified. As a result of this recommendation, in 2006 the Learning and Skills Development Agency (LSDA) evolved into two separate institutions: the Learning and Skills Network (LSN) which is responsible for research and development, and the Quality Improvement Agency for Lifelong Learning (QIA) which is responsible for commissioning quality improvement work, for example, new programmes and initiatives, in the Learning and Skills Sector.

Further, in 2006 the Leitch Report (DfES, 2006) examined the UK's long-term skills needs and included a proposal for a demand-led system of adult education with the aim of improving skills and strengthening the UK economy. In such a demand-led system the business community could stipulate their require-ments and have more of a say in vocational education and training provision. This would require what has now been termed 'employer engagement' by colleges and an emphasis on the economic functions of FE colleges at the expense of their social role. Training companies and skills brokers would be on the same footing as colleges in competing for vocational training contracts. As a result, it could be argued that the choice of vocational training given to students may be limited to that which is economically viable. Whatever the outcome, it is evident that the culture of the FE sector is already changing as a result of the Leitch Report, and the way students attend college and the way that you get students to learn will also have to change.

If you are aware of the policy issues in the FE sector and are aware of the reasons why students appear in your class and why they might be disgruntled, it is easier to understand what is going on and be more professional in your management of their learning and give consideration to the needs and concerns of students.

Changing practices

Harkin (2005: 166) intimates that there is a relatively new emphasis on the importance of the quality of teaching in FE, and in his discussion of professional development Harkin quotes Ofsted's view that successful colleges are characterized by the presence of self-critical, professional teachers:

> The most distinctive characteristic of these very good teachers is that their practice is the result of careful reflection, of advance planning which predicts what might occur and which accommodates the particular needs of all their students whose strengths and weaknesses they know intimately. Nothing is left to chance. Moreover they themselves also learn lessons each time they teach, evaluating what they do and using these self-critical evaluations to adjust what they do next time.
>
> (Ofsted, 2004: 9)

Academics and researchers, such as Harkin, influence the initial training of FE teachers and their professional development.

Harkin's response to Ofsted's view of 'good teachers' challenges the assumption that FE colleges are necessarily places that foster careful reflection. To support his claim, he draws on evidence from Schon (1983) which says that teachers who attempt reflective practice struggle against the rigidity of lesson plans, schedules, isolated classrooms and objective measures of performance. Although Ofsted obviously found evidence of 'careful reflection' and 'self-critical evaluations' by good teachers in successful colleges, the question Harkin raises is whether this is possible across the FE sector as his research findings are that 'many teachers said they had no time for reflection in their full-time teaching role' (Harkin, 2005). It would, therefore, be very difficult for them to learn lessons each time they teach, as Ofsted reported that the 'good teachers' did.

Academics and researchers explore difficult areas of teaching and learning and attempt to provide explanations that FE teachers can read about and apply to practice. Although the outcome of reflective practice by FE teachers implies the ability to adjust what they do next time, this is most successful when teachers' experiences enable them to develop personal theories and make judgements about adjusting practice when incorporating these personal theories. When FE teachers encounter new experiences or problems in a fast-changing sector they can draw on their own personal theories and deliberate about the things that are different, but really need to share their concerns with colleagues or collaborate with them in adapting practice and not attempt to critically reflect in isolation.

When you are at the end of your tether about some aspect of professional practice or having a panic about how to deal with changes in teaching and learning, it is nice to get a bit of advice from someone else and a great source of advice is to be found in textbooks written for teachers. Some are explicitly written for teachers in the FE sector, such as Ecclestone's (2002) excellent source of information about formative assessment, and the books for those training to teach in colleges (Minton, 2005; Rogers, 2002, 2003), but even so you have to apply the contents to your own context. It is inevitable that you tend to value textbooks that reflect your beliefs about education and read books by authors who think in similar ways to you. When faced with a problem in the classroom or workshop it is comforting to know that authors have already addressed similar issues and are willing to share their ideas in print. If their suggested solutions make sense to you, they can change the way you think about your problem and help you take appropriate action.

Hillier's (2005) textbook on reflective teaching is specifically addressed to the FE sector and widely used to inform practice on courses of initial training for teachers in FE (Harkin, 2005), but when you need to work out how to resolve problems with students' learning, you can adapt and interpret textbooks not specifically written for the FE sector. A good example of this is the way I have interpreted Pollard's (2002) theoretical frameworks and models. These were developed for use in schools but they are consistent with notions of reflection and evidence-informed practice which can be adapted for use in colleges and for FE students. You don't have time to start from scratch or start 're-inventing the wheel'. Nevertheless, every theory or standpoint needs to be adapted to your context and interpreted by you if it is to prove useful in improving practice. As an experienced FE teacher, I still rely on others to provide ideas to help me out of difficulties I face when I encounter new approaches to teaching and learning. The other titles in the Essential FE Toolkit Series are excellent sources of up-to-date, helpful information specifically written for FE teachers and are well worth reading.

Professional learning

Evidence-informed practice does not have to be restricted to academics and professional researchers. You can engage in action-research projects with like-minded colleagues, but try not to pick problems that you can't do much to change as a group of FE teachers. Focus on small things that have the potential to be changed and concentrate on improving teaching and learning. Being involved in small-scale action-research projects is a rewarding way of overcoming problems brought about by changing policies, and if you are open-minded enough to

117

constructively critique your own practices in collaboration with colleagues, as Stenhouse (1975) advocates, professional learning will result as he contends that teachers learn professionally through the critical practice of their art.

Professional learning doesn't mean you have to be surrounded by books or on the internet all the time. You can keep up-to-date with changes in your vocational area when visiting employers or assessing students in the workplace. Observing what is going on in the organization, having 'learning conversations' with employers or supervisors about your trainees, and discussing the latest techniques, products or practices as part of the student's evaluation can be extremely valuable ways of learning. Attending conferences or training days is another enjoyable way to keep up-to-date. Many events encourage you to join in group discussion or seminars and organize question and answer sessions when you can ask experts about things that are new to you or about to change. Chatting to other delegates over a relaxing meal or during a coffee break is another stimulating way of keeping abreast of what's going on in vocational education and training. In college you can ask to 'sit in' on experienced colleagues' sessions, or suggest you combine groups and get a member of the team who has got particular expertise to teach a part of the curriculum that has changed.

Perhaps you'll consider some of the ways you can engage in professional learning and find that it's not only essential to keep up-to-date because policies and practice are changing in the FE sector, but that it is an enjoyable experience as well.

Getting the buggers to learn: Focusing on professional learning

- Change is inevitable and you need to keep up-to-date in your subject and teaching methods;
- Develop your own personal theories about teaching and learning;
- Put your own ideas into practice as much as you can;
- Share ideas and problems with colleagues as much as possible;

- Collaborate in small-scale action-research projecta to develop evidence-informed practice;
- Don't be afraid of using others' ideas to help you deal with educational change;
- Remember the classroom is a key place for teachers to learn, not just students.

CONCLUSION

Focus on what matters

Formal schedule teaching, tutorials, student assessment, management of learning programmes and curriculum development, student admissions, educational guidance, counselling, preparation of learning materials and student assignments, marking student work, marking examinations, management and supervision of student visit programmes, research and other forms of scholarly activity, marketing activities, consultancy, leadership, supervisory, administration and personal professional development.

(Huddleston and Unwin, 2007: 25)

The above extract is from an employment contract of an FE teacher in one of the largest FE colleges in England, and illustrates what Huddleston and Unwin call the 'extraordinary' range of duties they will be expected to undertake. The diversity of an FE teacher's practice means that it is not easy for you to get your priorities right. In the Introduction to this book, Gleeson (2005) suggested that the FE learning experience was not a simple process for students and they had to balance their studies with other personal priorities. What I am suggesting as you reach the Conclusion of this book is that it is no easier for you to balance your teaching with other personal priorities. A juggling act is required to focus on what is important in your teaching, to enjoy your teaching and to sustain that vibrant lifestyle! You would need to be a magician to be able to conjure up more time every week, so what you have to do is to use the time you have wisely and focus on what matters.

You only have so much drive and energy and, just like students, your motivation fluctuates over the college year. You may start off with sessions all prepared, resources ready and a tidy desk, but towards the end of the year the pressure gets to you and you become jaded. Everybody gets anxious about marking, assessing outcomes and reaching targets. Dealing with difficult and disruptive students does get you down. As Huddleston and Unwin illustrate, your range of duties is extraordinary. Don't fall into the trap of making work for yourself. Share ideas and resources with colleagues and use the services of other professionals in the college, for example, counsellors, financial advisers, registrars, librarians or learning-support assistants, to deal with the range of problems students can face with learning and attending college.

I suggested in the Introduction that to survive in the classroom and enjoy your teaching you would have to change. FE teachers need to adopt many new roles and you may be a 'manager of resources', 'liaison officer for outside agencies', 'adviser', 'external assessor' or 'counsellor' according to Minton (2005: 211) but he urges FE teachers to 'approach their changing roles in all these capacities with a view of themselves primarily as teachers' and his advice would be well worth taking. If you view yourself primarily as a teacher your priorities become clear. I am not saying that this doesn't mean that you don't need to change or adopt new roles because to get students to learn you need to be flexible and adaptable in a sector of education that is changeable and frequently unpredictable.

Reflective practice, it is suggested, is a way of finding a link between thinking about a professional problem and taking personal action to improve: it is about making sense of professional life – its context, values, practice and ways of improving (Ghaye and Ghaye, 1998). However, it is difficult to reflect on your own and you probably just get downhearted. Reflection won't solve everything, but to work out how to balance the demands on your time and how to deal with conflicting priorities you really need to talk to others. So, I have taken the liberty of posing questions to you about 'getting the buggers to learn' in each chapter in the book – and provided some answers – but what I would like you to do is to respond to the questions and discuss them with colleagues with your own college in mind, your own classroom, your own students. In this way you can bring your own context, values and practice to ways of improving.

Guidelines for getting the buggers to learn

The following guidelines are drawn from the ideas presented in each chapter of this book and summarize my suggested approach for 'getting the buggers to learn in FE'.

---

1. FOCUS ON LEARNING
   Talk about learning to students
   Get students organized
2. FOCUS ON SUCCESS
   Get motivated through a series of short activities
   Give practical feedback and praise
3. FOCUS ON THE ENVIRONMENT
   Evaluate the classroom or your teaching area
   Resolve dilemmas with colleagues
   Work ethically and remember your values
4. FOCUS ON DEVELOPING IDEAS
   Identify personal theories
   Scaffold to develop potential
   Use assessment as learning
5. FOCUS ON STUDENTS
   Demonstrate empathy
   Develop rapport
   Encourage student control
6. FOCUS ON TEACHING
   Support and challenge
   Thoughtfully plan sessions
   Celebrate difference
7. FOCUS ON WHAT MATTERS
   Accept that change is always with us
   Be aware of policy changes
   Take an interest in research into practice
   Focus on professional learning

The seven points above combine to provide a strategy for you to implement with your students if you choose. For this to be successful you really need to listen to your students, talk to them and get to know them. Your role is to provide expertise, support, opportunities and encouragement so that students can help themselves to achieve what they want and need. This is why continuing with your own professional learning is essential, why it is worth the effort to develop competence in 'getting the buggers to learn in FE'.

REFERENCES

Armitage, A., Bryant, R., Dunnil, R., Renwick, M., Hayes, D., Hudson, A., Kent, J. and Lawes, S. (2003) *Teaching and Training in Post-Compulsory Education* (2nd edn). Maidenhead: Open University Press.

Bruner, J. (1990) *Acts of Meaning*. Cambridge, MA: Harvard University Press.

Cockburn, J. (2005) 'Perspectives and Politics of Classroom Observation', *Research in Post-Compulsory Education*, 10(3), pp. 373–88.

Covey, S. (1989) *The 7 Habits of Highly Effective People*. London: Simon and Schuster UK Ltd.

Department of Education and Skills (2006) *Prosperity for All in the Global Economy: World Class Skills*. Leitch Review of Skills. London: HMSO.

Drago-Severson. E. (2004) *Becoming Adult Learners: Principles and Practices for Effective Development*. New York: Teachers College Press.

Dweck, C. (1999) *Self-Theories: Their Role in Motivation, Personality and Development*. Philadelphia: Psychology Press.

Earl, M. (2003) *Assessment as Learning: Using Classroom Assessment to Maximise Student Learning*. Thousand Oaks, CA: Corwin Press.

Ecclestone, K. (2002) *Learning Autonomy in Post-16 Education: The politics and practice of formative assessment*. London: Routledge-Falmer.

Eisner, E. (1985) *The art of educational evaluation: a personal view*. London: Falmer Press.

Elliott, J. (1991) *Action Research for Educational Change*. Buckingham: Open University Press.

Foster, A. (2005) *Realizing the Potential: A review of the future role of further education colleges*. www.dfes.gov.uk/furthereducation/fereview

Ghaye, T. and Ghaye, K. (1998) *Teaching and Learning through Critical Reflective Practice*. London: David Fulton Publishers.

Gibson, R. (1986) *Critical Theory and Education*. London: Hodder and Stoughton.

Gleeson, D. (2005) 'Learning for a Change in Further Education', *Journal of Vocational Education and Training*, 57(2), pp. 239–46.

Gregory, J. (2002) 'Assessment of Experiental Learning in Higher Education', in P. Jarvis (ed.), *The Theory and Practice of Teaching*. London: Kogan Page.

Hager, P. (2005) 'The Competence Affair, or Why Vocational Education and Training Urgently Needs a New Understanding of Learning', *Journal of Vocational Education and Training*, 56(3), pp. 409–33.

Hanson, A. (1996) 'The search for a separate theory of adult learning: does anyone really need andragogy?' in R. Edwards, A. Hanson and P. Raggatt (eds), *Boundaries of Adult Learning*. London: Routledge/Open University Press.

Harkin, J. (2005) 'Fragments Stored against My Ruin: the place of educational theory in the professional development of teachers in further education', *Journal of Vocational Education and Training*, 57(2), pp. 165–79.

Hellriegel, D., Slocum, J. and Woodman, R. (1998) 'The Organizational Iceberg', in L. Mullins (1999), *Management and Organizational Behaviour* (5th edition). London: Financial Times-Pitman.

Hicks, L. (1999) 'The Nature of Learning', in L. Mullins, *Management and Organizational Behaviour* (5th edition). London: Financial Times-Pitman.

Hillier, Y. (2005) *Reflective Teaching in Further and Adult Education*. London: Continuum.

Hoare, S. (2007) 'Colleges Make it Personal', *The Guardian*, 9 January.

Hoban, G. (2002) *Teacher Learning for Educational Change*. Buckingham: Open University Press.

Houle, C. (1961) *The Inquiring Mind*. Madison: University of Wisconsin Press.

Huddleston, P. and Unwin, L. (2007) *Teaching and Learning in Further Education: Diversity and change* (3rd edition). London: Routledge.

Jarvis, P. (ed.) (2002) *The Theory and Practice of Teaching*. London: Kogan Page.

Jarvis, P., Holford, J. and Griffin, C. (1998) *Theory and Pracitce of Learning*. London: Routledge.

Jones, C. (2005) *Assessment for Learning.* London: Learning and Skills Development Agency.

Knowles, M. (1980) *The Modern Practice of Adult Education: From Pedagogy to Andragogy* (2nd edition). New York: Cambridge Books.

Leach, J. (2006) 'The Personal Touch', *Education Guardian.* London: The Guardian, 3 January 2006.

Marton, F., Hounsell, D. and Entwistle, N (eds) (1984) *The Experience of Learning.* Edinburgh: Scottish Academic Press.

Maslow, A. (1968) *Towards a Psychology of Being.* New York: Van Nostrand.

Minton, D. (2005) *Teaching Skills in Further and Adult Education* (3rd edition). London: Thomson Learning.

Morrison, M. (2005) 'E-learning 'Bites' for Adult Learners: mixed messages from research', *Research in Post-Compulsory Education,* 10(3), pp. 403–22.

Mullins, L. (1999) *Management and Organizational Behaviour* (5th edition). London: Financial Times-Pitman.

Ofsted (2004) Annual Report 2002–3. www.ofsted.gov.uk

Petty, G. (2004) *Teaching Today: A Practical Guide* (3rd edition). Cheltenham: Nelson Thornes.

Pollard, A. (2002) *Reflective Teaching: Effective and Evidence-informed Professional Practice.* London: Continuum.

Richardson, V. (1992) 'The agenda-setting dilemma in a constructivist staff development process', *Teaching and Teacher Education,* 8(3): 287–300.

Rogers, A (2002) *Teaching Adults* (3rd edition). Buckingham: Open University Press.

Rogers, A. (2003) *What is the Difference? A new critique of adult learning and teaching.* Leicester: Niace.

Rogers, C. (1983) *Freedom to Learn for the 1980s.* Columbus: Merril.

Rowntree, D. (1987) *Assessing Students: How shall we know them?* London: Kogan Page.

Rudduck, Flutter and Peddar *et al.* (2005) *Consulting pupils about teaching and learning.* http://www.standards.dfes.gov.uk/personalizedlearning (accessed 17 August 2007).

Schon, D. (1983) *The Reflective Practitioner: how professionals think in action.* London: Temple Smith.

Simkins, T. (1998) 'Autonomy, Constraint and the Strategic Management of Resources', in D. Middlewood and J. Lumby, *Strategic Management in Schools*. London: Paul Chapman.

Stenhouse, L. (1967) *Culture and Education*. London: Nelson Books.

Stenhouse, L. (1975) *An Introduction to Curriculum Research and Development*. London: Heinemann.

Steward, A (2003) 'Towards Constructive Practice: Lecturers Workloads, Roles and Professional Development', Anglia Ruskin University, unpublished EdD thesis.

The Transforming Learning Cultures in FE Project (2005) 'Improving Learning in Further Education: a new, cultural approach', *Teaching and Learning: Research Briefing Number 12*. London: Teaching and Learning Research Programme.

Tickle, L. (2000) *Teacher Induction: The Way Ahead*. Buckingham: Open University Press.

Tight, M. (ed.) (2000) *Academic Work and Life: What it is to be an academic, and how this is changing*. New York: Elsevier.

Visser, J. (2001) 'Integrity, completeness and comprehensiveness of the learning environment: meeting the basic learning needs of all through life', in D. Aspein *et al.* (eds), *International Handbook of Lifelong Learning*, pp. 610–44. London: Kluwer Academic Publishers.

Vygotsky, L. (1978) *Mind in Society*. London: Harvard University Press.

Wolcott, H. (2001) *Writing up Qualitative Research* (2nd edition). Thousand Oaks, CA: Sage.

Woods, P. (1996) *Researching the Art of Teaching: Ethnography for educational use*. London: Routledge.

INDEX